Colin Od

The Pocket Essential

TIM BURTON

www.pocketessentials.com

First published in Great Britain 2001 by Pocket Essentials, 18 Coleswood Road, Harpenden, Herts, AL5 1EQ

Distributed in the USA by Trafalgar Square Publishing, PO Box 257, Howe Hill Road, North Pomfret, Vermont 05053

A CIP catalogue record for this book is available from the British Library.

ISBN 1-903047-62-5

2 4 6 8 10 9 7 5 3 1

Book typeset by Pdunk
Printed and bound by Cox & Wyman

For Marc and Delphine

Acknowledgements

Our thanks to the usual suspects Paul, Lizbeth and Andy for the welcome distractions, apostrophes, accounting, gig bookings and movies. A big hello to Martin and Rosy (thanks for waiting for us while we edited this) and Ben and Heather (we will make it to one of your parties one day). Thanks to Andrea and Ian for finding cuttings for us. Domo arigato gozaimasu to Geoff, Steve and Veronica for all the karate training which led to our black belts. Thanks to our fab folks for all their support, as ever and especially to Mum for sending loads of clippings. A huge thank you to Jim next door, who has done wonderful things to our garden while we've been watching films and writing books. Finally to Alice Razorclaws, a most misunderstood and mischievous moggy.

CONTENTS

Tim Burton - Hollywood Contradiction 7

And It All Started Happily Ever After 15
*Vincent (1982), Hansel And Gretel (1982), Frankenweenie (1984),
Faerie Tale Theatre: Aladdin And His Wonderful Lamp (1984)*

Look Bike In Anger 23
Pee-wee's Big Adventure (1985)

It's Showtime! 29
The Jar (1985), Beetlejuice (1988)

Holy Budgets, Batman 35
Batman (1989)

An Uncommonly Gentle Man 42
Edward Scissorhands (1990)

Bats, Cats And An Army That Quacks 49
Batman Returns (1992)

Angora, Bela, Cinema: The ABC Of Ed Wood 55
Ed Wood (1994)

Do Not Run, We Are Your Friends 62
Mars Attacks! (1996)

Tackling The Classics Head On 68
Sleepy Hollow (1999)

Monkey Business 75
Planet Of The Apes (2001)

Other Skellingtons In The Closet - Burton As Producer 81
*Family Dog (1987-1993), The Nightmare Before Christmas (1993),
Cabin Boy (1994), Batman Forever (1995), James And The Giant
Peach (1996)*

What's This? Other Projects 88
Singles (1992), Adverts, Stainboy

Burton Books And Bookmarks 90
Books, DVDs, Videos and Websites

Tim Burton - Hollywood Contradiction

"It can't be Halloween every day you know."

"It is for me."

Beetlejuice Cartoons: Critter Sitters

Tim Burton is an artist. Normally such a statement is anathema to all that Hollywood cinema stands for. Hollywood, we are told, is a land where the only recognisable art is that on a dollar bill. How then can you explain the continued success of Tim Burton? His output is filled with imagery that is morbid or grotesque. He spends vast amounts of money directing films within genres that are either past their sell-by date or reserved for the straight-to-video market. He has produced a body of work that focuses on the outcasts of society. His villains are rarely resolutely evil - they're normally misunderstood. Traditional narrative techniques exist in his films, but are secondary to image and feeling. In some senses his output is belittled by mere description - a film about a man who has scissors instead of hands may sound trite but needs to be felt. It is the overall aesthetic cohesion that makes his work stand out. Conceptually he is far removed from the mainstream, and yet is successful enough to ensure that his name on a film is eminently marketable.

Although often seen as deeply shy, withdrawn, sensitive and unwilling to face confrontation, Tim Burton is nonetheless shrewd when it comes to business. In this respect his path as a director seems to follow both commercial and personal projects – the more money he has to work with, the more profitable the studios expect his finished product to be. He doesn't intentionally waste studio money, but follows his instincts as to what he would like to see. Fortunately this is a body of work that is sumptuous and steeped in arresting imagery. The downside of this is the infrequency of new Burton films – the project must be right and the studios willing to cough up the cash – but it's a price worth paying for what is undoubtedly one of Hollywood's most fascinating directors.

Although Tim Burton's oeuvre connects with a large portion of the cinema-going audience, he is ostensibly a mainstream cult director. As such, his more personal films have little market outside his niche audience - fortunately for him and the studios that niche is sufficiently large. However, his films must make a profit, which makes his position as one of Hollywood's leading A-list directors a fragile one. This is an inherent problem; his most financially successful films are also his weakest artistically. He needs money to realise his personal vision but if the box office does not show healthy returns, he faces loss of control and dilution of the very thing that makes his work so

7

interesting. The current climate has meant that his last two films, *Sleepy Hollow* and *Planet Of The Apes*, were hits; *Sleepy Hollow* also remaining, quintessentially, an uncompromised Burton film. His previous two films, *Mars Attacks!* and *Ed Wood*, failed to recoup their costs despite the former being popular in Europe and the latter winning an Oscar.

Gothic Trappings, Nonsense Rhymes And Macabre Etchings

What makes a Burton film so magical is the influence of past absurdities and eccentricities, the never-never land of children's books or the charnel house trappings of the existential horror writers. The links between horror, folk tale and fantasy genres have always been strong, especially in the world of children. There is a time in their life when they can confront their worst fears, where everything is understood but nothing is impossible. It is the duality of the magically wonderful and grotesquely grim, the soul torn between wonder and despair. This is the world of Tim Burton. His literary heritage stems from Walpole's *The Castle Of Otranto* to the melancholy despair of Edgar Allan Poe. It's a world of waking dreams and delirium. Unlike filmmakers who develop along the path of surrealism and touch upon horror or the bizarre, Burton adopts a different route that takes in the feel of Lewis Carroll (frightening but detached), the Brothers Grimm and Edward Lear. The influence of Dr Seuss, both in rhyming and illustration cannot be ignored - the spindly creatures, striped hats and mischief makers who retain sympathy, feed directly into Burton's body of work. Closest of all aesthetically is Edward Gorey, writer, artist and designer whose quirky, macabre books contain more than a hint of the Burtonesque with misunderstood individuals (including the moping, unwanted penguin-looking creature of *The Doubtful Guest*) inside a world of Edwardian angst. This goes a long way to explain the rare filmic charm of Burton's work - his heritage as a film-maker differs from that of his peers because his output descends from phantasmagorical tales so beloved of pre-cinema magic lantern shows. In telling fables or allegorical stories there is very little visual subtext to much of his work - the tale is told in a fantastical light and not burdened with too much extraneous baggage. This economy makes his best films timeless and hits the basic human emotions, as all good folk tales should. Burton is a fantasy film-maker - fantasy refers here to the fantastic rather than the sword 'n' sandal/sorcery/elves sense of the term - and even his horror films *Mars Attacks!* and *Sleepy Hollow* do not scare in the conventional ways associated with the genre. They are the embodiment of a nostalgic youth – the wonder of discovery – like opening up a musty book on a windy night and being unsure as to what's inside.

Themes And Motifs

"I'm a loner. A rebel."

Pee-wee Herman in Pee-wee's Big Adventure

It normally does not take more than a few seconds of screen time to realise that you are watching a Burton movie. This is because he employs a number of recurring themes and motifs that create a cohesive and personal vision. In some senses you are not watching a Tim Burton film, but entering his world.

Genre Subversion: The key to Burton's approach with his film projects lies in the way he takes an established genre and twists it. By confounding expectations, particularly in the mainstream where audiences are used to formulaic films, he creates a sense of wonder and discovery. In *Beetlejuice* the concept of the haunted house film is subverted - instead of eccentric, macabre ghosts haunting a bland family, a horrible family haunt a pair of bland ghosts. The biopic *Ed Wood* concentrates on someone who was, arguably, not at all successful. The *Batman* films focus more on the villains, the hero himself being of a dubious nature and psychologically scarred. In *Batman Returns* Burton pulls off the impressive trick of making you care for a physically repulsive, lecherous freak who wants to slaughter an entire city's child population. *Mars Attacks!* sees us rooting for the aliens to destroy Earth and features a president who doesn't rally his troops *Henry V* style into patriotic war, but is totally ineffectual. *Edward Scissorhands* sees the teen romance film twisted by having the main romantic lead an automata with more heart than any human. *Sleepy Hollow* has a hero coroner who can't bear the sight of blood and *Pee-wee's Big Adventure* subverts the comedy genre by having a central character who isn't funny!

Classic Horrors and B-Flicks: Many of Burton's films use the look of classic science fiction and horror movies, particularly those of the 1950s and 1960s, as a template for his visual style. Among the films that seem to have influenced Burton are those produced by Roger Corman, as well as Mario Bava. Bava is the stylish Italian film-maker whose works include *The Mask Of Satan* (a big influence on *Sleepy Hollow)* as well as a series of garish serial killer films such as *Blood And Black Lace* and *Bay Of Blood*. The techniques employed by animators Ray Harryhausen and Willis O'Brien are a big influence, and the attraction of period horror films produced by Hammer is also clear.

Angst And The Outsider: In many respects Tim Burton films are about not fitting into society, about people who don't conform with the attitudes and mores of the day. This concept of the misanthropic person, normally a youth, comes from a number of sources; there is the association with Burton himself, the fascination with self-loathing that Edgar Allan Poe explored, and the angst-ridden Gothic aesthetic of his films. Perhaps this helps connect his body of work with so many young people who feel disenfranchised with society and relate to the characters they see on the screen. The most sympathetically portrayed protagonists are those who differ from the norm - be they awkward, gauche, naive or simply misunderstood.

Characters' Origins: The origins of a character, particularly concerning their parents (or lack of them), form a significant contribution to their psyche. Pee-wee apparently has no parents or any guiding authority figure and acts as such - he has no responsibility. Batman's bereavement and The Penguin's rejection lead them in diametrically opposed directions morally, but there is no doubt that both lives would have been radically different without that parental loss. This theme comes to the fore in *Edward Scissorhands* and *Sleepy Hollow*. Structurally and traumatically Edward's origins are similar to that of Ichabod Crane. In both films we learn about their pasts via a series of flashbacks which terminate in the event that shaped the central character - the death of a loving parent. In *Edward Scissorhands* this death is moving and shocking as young Edward cannot understand what has happened to his creator. In *Sleepy Hollow* the death isn't melancholy or dignified but horrific, deliberately instigated to instil fear. What both Edward and Ichabod have learnt from their departed (good) parents is treated very differently. Ichabod rejects all faith, but eventually turns back and accepts that of his mother, while Edward, having no other source of information about society, can only rely upon the etiquette his creator taught him. Even when sympathetic characters do have parents (Lydia in *Beetlejuice*, Richie and Taffy in *Mars Attacks!*) they are inattentive to their children's needs and it would probably be better that they were absent altogether.

The Bastard Sons Of Frankenstein: Mad scientists and mad science populate many of the narratives - young Victor Frankenstein, Edward Scissorhands' Inventor, Ichabod Crane, the Martian technicians, Alfred the butler, Vincent Malloy and Jack Skellington all have traits that are shared with Mary Shelley's most renowned scientist. The results of their labours and those of unseen creators (such as the inventor of Pee-wee's breakfast machine) contribute to both the drive of the narratives and ambience of the films.

Disrespect Of Authority: Figures of authority rarely get a good time. They are symbolic of the status quo and thus not to be trusted. The exception to this is *Edward Scissorhands* where the policeman is one of the few people who realises the extent of Edward's problems and attempts to protect him from the angry mob, but such instances are rare. More common are the authorities being ridiculed or seen as actively evil. In *Batman* the mayor is a useless figure. In *Batman Returns* the true evil person is not the Penguin but entrepreneur Max Shreck. In *Mars Attacks!* the President is incompetent, his rich wife vacuous and again the businessman is portrayed as uncouth. In S*leepy Hollow* judges and policemen doubt the validity of Ichabod's deductive reasoning, as do the respectable leaders of the country community.

The Grotesque: Whether it is the evil rays of the Martians, the resurrection of a dead dog, the autopsy of a pregnant cadaver, the tragic death of a young boy's creator, dribbling bile from the mouth of a deformed man, evil clowns with nasty surgical tools or the headless horsemen clutching a bag of heads, there is always something grotesque going on. This is closely linked with his morbid themes, but what makes Burton's work so unusual is that the use of such devices does not make for depressing viewing. It is another contradiction. His films deal with the sinister and macabre but somehow manage to be uplifting examples of entertainment.

Stripes and Swirls: Burton's films are remarkably visual, which comes as no surprise bearing in mind his origins as an animator and artist. His style is apparent in the design of his films and the mise en scène he employs - the stripy sock sand worms of *Beetlejuice*, the swirls covering the Martian spy girl's dress and Jack Skellington's impossibly spiralling hilltop upon which he expresses his woes. Every Burton film bears visual embellishments, which emanate from his original pre-production sketches.

Weird Sciences And Domestic Appliances: Gadgets are part of every superhero's arsenal and every boy's dream. From the elaborate breakfast-making devices in Pee-wee's house to the kitsch but fully functional cookie machine of *Edward Scissorhands*, machinery plays a large part in shaping not only the characters, but their relationship with the outside world. Batman's inability to communicate is shown in his over-reliance on gadgets, from his costume to the Batmobile - they're all safely stashed away in the cavernous recesses of Wayne Mansion. The Martians are similarly attached to their toys and technology - they are spoilt rich kids, amoral versions of Batman, relishing their technological supremacy. They share similar traits with that of the Inventor, creating new things out of old, for an unclear purpose. Even in *Sleepy Hollow* Ichabod has all the latest forensic equipment.

> "I'm of that generation where, you know, I'm polluted by television"

> Tim Burton (Behind the Scenes – Timex Commercials)

Television: Burton is a child of the television generation - indeed much of his film knowledge comes from reruns that, at the time, only the channel-heavy States could supply. It plays a massive role in imparting information, plot or character development, paradoxically providing a link with reality. Pee-wee learns of his bike's fate whilst watching television in hospital and Betelgeuse advertises his services on TV. The Joker's first major strike affects a newscaster and both the Penguin and Max Shreck use television as a propaganda tool to discredit Batman. In *Mars Attacks!* two central characters are presenters and the first indications of the Martians' destructive intentions are broadcast live across the globe. In *Ed Wood* television provides Ed with Vampira and gives Lugosi a humiliating break. A pivotal moment in *Edward Scissorhands* is when Edward appears on a chat show - at once we know why Edward is special, that he really does love Kim and that she realises this. In *Planet Of The Apes* the strange electromagnetic storm that is the catalyst for the adventure beams back television signals from a distant galaxy. Strangely, although television does not play a part in *Sleepy Hollow* (unsurprisingly), it does in *Aladdin*!

Snow: Snow plays a big part in the visual ideology within Burton's films. Aesthetically it is appealing yet also represents something that is often hated and can be deadly, cold and distant. *Sleepy Hollow* uses snow to represent key events in the little town's violent history and *Batman Returns* opens with snow at Christmas time - a season for celebration curtailed by the icy grip of a crime wave. But snow is not all bad. Edward Scissorhands brings the gift of magical snow to the town, and snow reflects his moment of pure happiness when he realises that Kim loves him.

Dogs: Burton is fascinated by dogs. In fact one of his designs led to the animated series *Family Dog*. The love of Sparky in *Frankenweenie* is such that its young owner is driven to resurrect him from the dead. Speck appears as Pee-wee's dog and the Maitlands in *Beetlejuice* die in an accident because a mischievous mutt jumped off the plank that was keeping their car precariously balanced on a bridge. *Edward Scissorhands* features a whole neighbourhood of them waiting to be elegantly fur-styled while the unfortunate Nathalie in *Mars Attacks!* becomes attached to her hound in a far more macabre way - her head is swapped with her pooch's.

Godzilla: For aficionados there is nothing better than a Godzilla film (and we're not talking about that dreadful Hollywood travesty we mean the real Toho beast). In fact Burton once said he would like to have played Godzilla trampling models of Tokyo. And who can blame him? It is no coincidence that this image crops up in many of Burton's films - from Edward Scissorhands' topiary to the conclusion of *Pee-wee's Big Adventure,* as well as the Big G himself appearing on television in *Mars Attacks!*

Tim Burton: A common figure to see in a Burton film is that of Tim Burton, or rather an idealised version of himself. Many of his films feature some character that seems to represent Tim and his upbringing. For example, the pale-skinned, unruly-haired protagonist of *Vincent*, the character of Lydia in *Beetlejuice*, Edward Scissorhands, and Richie in *Mars Attacks*.

Style

Stylistically Burton is undeniably Hollywood's most distinctive mainstream director. Every film is designed to within an inch of its life, with the mise en scène and visual motifs providing so much of what should be considered typical Burton. There is undoubtedly a wide variation in the look of his films. Both *Pee-wee's Big Adventure* and *Mars Attacks!* employ bright and vivid Day-Glo colours, to indicate extremities of scale. Alternatively, in his moribund Gothic films, gloom and despondency are similarly reflected in the colour schemes. In *Batman* and *Batman Returns*, despite occasionally garish use of colour, the predominant palette of the film is dark, almost black & white or sepia in tone, reflecting Batman's brooding nature. With *Ed Wood* the black & white film stock gives a sentimental feel and provides a degree of nostalgic realism, which is appropriate in a biopic. *Sleepy Hollow* has a tinted feel - muted autumnal colours which complement the dead forest and creepy mist.

Expressionism is fundamental to the Burton ethos and many of the classics of early German cinema seem to have had an effect on his work, perhaps because of the saturation of images that came from these influential films. In particular *The Cabinet Of Dr Caligari* (1919) with its twisted sets, forced perspective backdrops and use of psychological realism over material realism sees reflection in a number of Burton's scenes. Of particular note are the underground cavern in *Aladdin And His Wonderful Lamp*, the bike surgery sequence from *Pee-wee's Big Adventure*, the Netherworld from *Beetlejuice*, the tortured appearance of *Edward Scissorhands* and Gotham City's awe-inspiring architecture. This is emphasised by the fact that most of his productions are not filmed on location but on studio sets, often at great expense, which allows Burton complete control to realise these stunning visual ideas.

In terms of film-making techniques, Burton's means of telling a story is fairly conventional and based around traditional Hollywood methods. Most of his narratives are linear, as befits the telling of a faerie tale or fable, although he does incorporate bookending devices and flashbacks. In many of his works (particularly *Pee-wee's Big Adventure*, *Beetlejuice*, *Mars Attacks*, *Ed Wood* and even *Planet Of The Apes*) there is an almost gleeful disregard for narrative pacing - events form apparently freestyle and merge from one to another. In this respect some of his films have the lucidity of a road movie (in *Pee-wee's* case literally as well as structurally). Burton rarely employs tension or suspense, which is unusual for works within the horror genre. However, he punctuates the flow of the films with tangential flourishes. One of these is the Large Marge shot, the sudden scare, as seen in *Pee-wee's Big Adventure*. Pee-wee is picked up by a bulky lorry driver who tells him the terrible tale of "the worst accident I'd ever seen. When they pulled the driver's body from the burning twisted wreck, it looked like this" before turning to a terrified Pee-wee, her eyes out on their stalks, her tongue lolling around and her hair a massive shock of matted fury. It's a shot that gets repeated in *Beetlejuice* as well as *Sleepy Hollow*. Although quite shocking, its value is purely comedic.

With the exception of *Ed Wood*, all Burton's features have been scored by the incredible Danny Elfman. His distinctive music perfectly complements the images on screen - be they manic, ethereal or haunting. His rhythms can be full of purpose or incredibly complex and his melodies eminently memorable. Elfman was part of a bizarre ensemble band called Oingo Boingo as guitarist, composer and singer. The band had grown partly out of his brother Richard and friends' avant-garde project The Mystic Knights Of The Oingo Boingo and was dedicated to anything remotely unfashionable. The Boingo's mix of jazz instrumentation with rock pop sensibilities weren't to everyone's taste but Burton was a huge fan and persuaded Elfman to come aboard for *Pee-wee's Big Adventure*. Elfman's manic music was a major step on the ladder of stardom that would see many more outstanding scores including Sam Raimi's *Darkman* and Warren Beatty's *Dick Tracy* as well as *The Simpsons*.

And It All Started Happily Ever After

Timothy William Burton was born in Burbank, California, on August 25, 1958. Burbank is the essence of American middle-class suburbia and also home to many of the major film studios, the combination of which would have a huge effect on Burton. At school his academic record was unremarkable although he did win a poster competition for litter prevention. Young Burton found it difficult to relate to the conformist community in which he lived and turned to films as a means of escape. His imagination was inspired by pulp and exploitation films, movies deemed to be lowbrow, cheesy or devoid of artistic merit. He watched horror, science fiction and anything that featured Godzilla or his favourite actor Vincent Price. Price was a veteran of many a horror flick, but was particularly known for the series of Edgar Allan Poe adaptations made by low-budget supremo Roger Corman in the 1960s. Films such as *The Pit And The Pendulum* (1961 - an influence on *Sleepy Hollow*), *Tomb Of Ligeia* (1964) and *The Masque Of The Red Death* (1963) were a combination of colourful widescreen spectacle and morbid obsession with death and decay. This contrast of colour and darkness, art and pulp would fuel Burton's own body of work.

Whilst still at school Burton experimented with filming using a Super-8 camera. Like Steven Spielberg and John Carpenter these juvenilia were predominantly science fiction films, monster movies of the sort that took his imagination. Escapism. He also experimented with stop-motion animation in the manner of the great Ray Harryhausen, whose wonderful effects techniques would inspire the look of the Martians in *Mars Attacks!*. Burton would take his animation further. At the age of 18 he found himself admitted to the California Institute of the Arts having won a scholarship. CalArts was founded by Disney as a means of helping young animators and directors learn their trade. It was a two-way thing. The students would get the education they needed and Disney could pick from the cream of the crop. Burton was recognised as a talent and taken out of CalArts prematurely to work for them.

At that time Disney was in turmoil. Walt's death had led to a number of ill-founded decisions and a relentless spate of insipid films. But this state of confusion in the Mouse House would ultimately prove beneficial for Burton. His first assignment was on the animated feature *The Fox And The Hound* (1981), a rather bland buddy flick. He was ill-suited for the project because his skills as an artist were not in tune with its inherent cuteness - his own attempts looked like, in his own words, "roadkills." Realising that he was not getting on well with the Disney ethos he was given a job as a conceptual artist, designing characters and ideas for use in future projects. One of these was *The Black Cauldron* (released 1985). On the surface this seemed like an ideal avenue to channel Burton's more outré talents, being concerned with magic, strange creatures and bizarre contraptions, but it was not to be. Burton's drawings from this period are bursting with ideas. The scratchy, fevered sketches, as though from an ancient bestiary, are quirky, macabre but strangely endearing. It was around this time that he first drew Jack Skellington, which was the genesis of *The Nightmare Before Christmas*. Despite the obvious talent behind the ideas, it was again decided that Burton's concepts were at odds with the film, so ultimately none of the sketches were fleshed out into the final production. Instead of continually throwing unsuitable projects at him, Disney gave him $60,000 to make a short animated film based on his own writing and drawings which he had originally intended to be published as a children's book. Teaming up with fellow CalArts colleague Rick Heinrichs he used a blend of model and cel animation to realise the vision.

"Vincent Malloy is seven years old

He's always polite and does what he's told

For a boy his age he's considerate and nice

But he wants to be just like Vincent Price"

Tim Burton - *Vincent*

Vincent (1982)

Crew: Dir: Tim Burton, Prd: Rick Heinrichs, 6 mins
Cast: Vincent Price

Plot: Young Vincent lives in his house with his mother, sister and pets. But this life is far too normal and Vincent prefers to play in his fantasy world, where he paints and reads Edgar Allan Poe. He dreams about dipping his aunt in wax, creating a horrible zombie from his dog and digs his mother's flower bed up - searching for his buried wife, you understand. His mother is particularly perturbed by his peculiarly plaintive perspective and insists that he go out and play in the sun. But Vincent doesn't want to. He'd rather mooch about the house in melancholy mood, being morbid.

Comment: Originally intended as a children's story and a tribute to Burton's hero, *Vincent* came about as a result of Disney's generosity, when his superiors Julie Hickson and Tom Wilhite realised that young Burton needed to find a creative direction. This delightful five-minute short employs an unusual combination of cel animation and stop-motion model work. Shot in black and white, the film contains a number of unusual stylistic embellishments, many of which would find their way into Burton's later work.

It is impossible not to compare Vincent with Burton himself - the quiet, shy boy with masses of unruly hair, who is only truly comfortable inside his fertile imagination. What is so striking about the film is that it deals with themes that crop time and again within Burton's oeuvre: the young boy's rejection of the environment in which he lives, grotesque fantasies about doing evil things to his relations and the mad young scientist in his laboratory. Vincent himself has such style - he smokes cigarettes through a holder with panache and experiments feverishly in his bedroom lab wearing large black gloves and a white coat. It is only when elements of normality enter his world that he becomes a disconsolate ordinary little boy. Indeed every transition from Vincent Malloy to Vincent Price is wonderfully executed, the scale within his world reflecting his current state of mind. Everything is filmed from a seven-year-old's viewpoint - adults are identifiable by their legs and furniture is scaled appropriately. When Vincent sits at his desk to write, his tiny head and hands are dwarfed by the enormous quill in the foreground. Burton's use of perspective is remarkable.

The film reflects Burton's love of horror films and literature and is filled to the brim with references - *Fall Of The House Of Usher*, *House Of Wax*, *Frankenstein* and *Nosferatu*. Also remarkable was the involvement of Vincent Price himself - the studio sent the storyboards to Price who was immediately impressed with the charm of the story and agreed to provide the voice-over. The opportunity to work with his childhood hero must have been a significant inspiration for Burton's future career.

Unfortunately, Disney were unimpressed with Burton's first film. They could not understand the concept of a little boy who was genuinely morbid and not 'redeemed' by the film's close. They wanted an upbeat ending, where Vincent becomes just like every other little boy. They missed the point. *Vincent* is a wonderful short which was not released by Disney at the time, but had to wait for Burton to become famous.

The Verdict: 5/5

Hansel And Gretel (1982)

Crew: Dir: Tim Burton, Prd & Scr: Julie Hickson, 45 mins
Cast: Michael Yama, Jim Ishida

Plot: Toy business in recession, hungry kids and a partner not conducive to the sound of tiny feet mean only one thing to siblings Hansel and Gretel - eviction from the family home by not entirely fair means. The wandering two-some come across a residence of a far more edible nature than their old home so that's all right, time to tuck into the masonry. But things are not always as they seem, as the owner of the sugary cottage is a witch with a taste for plump little kiddies. Yum, yum.

Comment: After *Vincent*, Burton was conscious that he needed to work with actors. With this in mind he pitched the concept of *Hansel And Gretel* to Disney as a show for their new cable service The Disney Channel. Naturally though, he was keen to add a twist to the proceedings and introduce some elements that interested him, particularly his love of Japanese films. The remit was to create *Hansel And Gretel* with an all-Japanese cast (their father's toy-shop is filled to the brim with Transformer toys - cool!), and could end the programme with a big martial arts scrap between the children and the witch. Inspired. The budget of $116,000 for the effects-laden script meant that some of the sequences were a touch hurried, but this often adds charm to proceedings. Again Heinrichs provided a myriad of different techniques to realise Burton's quirky drawings: the skewed candy-covered witch's house, some stop-frame work, front projections and a gingerbread puppet whose powers of persuasion are tested to the max forcing Hansel to eat him. The design for this puppet is similar to the Red Circus Gang Clowns in *Batman Returns* with wide, dead eyes and face-splitting grin. Burton emphasises the scary elements of faerie tales by including creatures gyrating out of cauldrons and a cross-dressing witch. Unfortunately, though this aspect has been a strong part of Disney's best work (*Snow White* or the 'Night On Bald Mountain' sequence from *Fantasia*), it is not something that has really survived the company's more 'wholesome' output. A shame, because the confrontational and mythical aspects of faerie tales are what gives them their power. *Hansel And Gretel* was shown on its intended channel. Once. Late at night. And then Disney locked it away. Where it remains today. Still, Burton learned how to deal with actors and proved he could film to specification which ultimately led to the greenlighting of his next project.

Frankenweenie (1984)

Crew: Dir: Tim Burton, Prd: Julie Hickson, Scr: Lenny Ripp from an idea by Tim Burton, 24 mins

Cast: Shelley Duvall (Susan Frankenstein), Daniel Stern (Ben Frankenstein), Barrett Oliver (Victor), Paul Bartel (Mr Walsh)

"We wanna be dog like Sparky."

Cardiacs

Plot: Introducing Sparky, part-time canine thespian, full-time loving companion to schoolboy Victor Frankenstein. And now, sadly, barking along with the choir invisible following a nasty incident involving a rubber ball and a fast moving vehicle. For most young boys this would be a time for grieving but, following an inspirational science lesson, Victor has a purpose. Digging up his deceased dog, Victor is determined to add credence to Sparky's name by hot-wiring him into the mains of Mother Nature and resurrecting the hound. Reunited, the pair couldn't be happier. Sparky is coming to terms with his neck bolts, Mrs Frankenstein is renewing her sewing skills on the dog's wounds and Victor is his old perky self once more. Such scenes of domestic bliss cannot last forever and, sure enough, the neighbourhood are not impressed by a pooch from beyond the grave. The neighbours are revolting and have Sparky in their sights, hounding him (so to speak) to almost certain death in a flaming windmill, determined to bring new meaning to the term 'hot dog'...

Comment: Despite Burton's assertion that given more time *Frankenweenie* could have been extended into a full-length movie, it is hard to see how additional material could have improved the piece - it remains a perfectly formed short that never outlives its welcome. *Frankenweenie* looks primarily to James Whale's *Frankenstein* (1931) and *Bride Of Frankenstein* (1935), with the twist that it all happens through a child's eyes. Instead of *Frankenstein's* conventional cemetery, *Frankenweenie* has a pet one with tombstones for the dearly departed, such as Bubbles the goldfish. The electric buzzing 'thing' so popular in mad scientist films has been cobbled together from an old blender. The lightning-capturing kite is replaced by a helium balloon and the university downgraded to a junior school. Even the windmill climax has been suitably scaled. The final reward for a good dog is a mate, which is just what lucky old Sparky gets at the film's close - a black poodle with an Elsa Lanchester white stripe in her fur! It's not only Universal films that get a look in - when it is revealed that Sparky is having problems with his stitches, Victor's mum comes to the rescue with a needle and thread, biting off the excess twine with her teeth rather like Peter Cushing in an altogether more visceral scene from Terence Fisher's *Frankenstein And The Monster From Hell* (1973). There are other nods too: Sparky stars in *Monsters From Long Ago*, a pastiche of Willis O'Brien's *The Lost World* (1925) and the live action Godzilla films; Paul Bartel gets to do the Dead Parrot sketch with an amphibian ("It is an ex-frog"); and there's even a car racing reference to *Rebel Without A Cause* (1955).

Victor's experiments resurrecting his dead pet continue the mad scientist theme that started in *Vincent* (his experimenting on the long-suffering Abercrombie) and continues in much of Burton's work. Victor's laboratory may look like his namesake's but is furnished with more mundane items such as toasters or blenders and started using an upside-down bike (although what Pee-wee would make of such sacrilege is anyone's guess). Victor himself is another Burton extension - a boy with a fascination for the macabre that society does not understand. His neighbours are the same as those in *Edward Scissorhands* in that they are reactionary and conservative. Like both Vincent and Edward, Victor has a sympathetic mother figure who, despite being thoroughly domestic, tries to accommodate his peculiarities.

Frankenweenie is impossible not to like - it is light, funny and feels good whilst paradoxically keeping all the morbid elements from *Frankenstein* intact. Disney were surprisingly impressed with the finished result and wanted to give the film a wide distribution alongside the reissue of *Pinocchio* (1940) as a showcase of Disney old and new. Wanted to but didn't. Unfortunately *Frankenweenie* was slapped with a PG rating by the Motion Picture Association of America which effectively prevented its distribution with the lower G-rated film. But again its qualities were recognised by people who counted, one of whom was Shelley Duvall. Duvall had long encouraged the works of up-and-coming directors and had set up a well regarded television series *Faerie Tale Theatre* which had a reputation for producing eccentric and innovative versions of well-known tales. She gave Burton another directing opportunity.

The Verdict: 5/5

Faerie Tale Theatre:
Aladdin And His Wonderful Lamp (1984)

Crew: Dir: Tim Burton, Exec Prd: Shelley Duvall, 44 mins

Cast: Robert Carradine (Aladdin), Valerie Bertinelli (Princess Sabrina), Leonard Nimoy (Moroccan Magician - boo hiss), Joseph Maher (Sultan), James Earl Jones (Genie of the Lamp/Genie of the Ring), Ray Sharkey (Grand Vizier)

"I don't think that man was your uncle"

"Of course not - he was an evil Moroccan magician"

Plot: Aladdin, lazy devil, bit of a prankster, sees the prospect of a life of prosperity in the shape of his hitherto unacquainted rich uncle. The fly in this ointment is that uncle is not an estranged relation but a scheming Moroccan mage with designs on purloining an ancient lamp with prodigious supernatural properties - a task he assigns to the eager young lad, promising immense wealth and the opportunity to establish a marble shop. However, at the climax of Aladdin's underground filching escapade, the boy realises the sorcerer's sham and retains the illuminating prize at the inconvenient cost of subterranean incarceration. Aladdin is resourceful and, on his escape, chances upon the reason for the lamp's high esteem - it contains a genie capable of granting his bidding. A simple life of luxury is assured but when Aladdin catches sight of Princess Sabrina, the fair daughter of the Sultan, he is besotted, raising his expectations to those of regal nuptials and he wins her hand. Pleasant espousal in sumptuous magical palace surroundings beckons, but there is a cloud on the horizon - the mightily miffed Moroccan Magician is determined to claim the magical lamp for his own, undoubtedly dubious, purposes and has a cunning plan. New lamps for old anyone?

Comment: Shelley Duvall's *Faerie Tale Theatre* (note the exemplary spelling) was a showcase for new talent that gave many up-and-coming people their first shot at the industry. Using a combination of well-respected actors and newcomers, the show retold children's faerie tales in a way that was innovative and non-patronising. To this end it was highly successful but its market limited primarily to the very young. Unfortunately, while innovation was encouraged, the productions were shot on videotape which does little to endear them on an aesthetic level. Also, shooting schedules in television land are very tight, especially considering that *Aladdin* is, by its very nature, an effects-heavy story (flying carpets, magical transportations, a mystical palace transported like a rocketship). In order to realise the project Burton brought along Rick Heinrichs to help construct the sets. There are many Burton touches in these backdrops - impossibly colourful skies, swirls on the sets and lines that are anything but straight.

It is easy to criticise the overall result but there is much to enjoy if you accept the limitations of the medium. The most remarkable scene occurs when Aladdin seeks to retrieve the lamp from an underground lair. Ordered not to touch the walls he crawls down a disjointed and ever diminishing expressionist corridor lined with skulls. Expectations from the establishing shot that this is forced perspective is curtailed by the subsequent side-on shot indicating that the perspective is real - it's a true Burton moment. Likewise when he reaches the chamber that contains the lamp, the walls are replete with Burton silhouettes (including a spiky precursor to *Family Dog*), rather like the phantasmagorical spooks from the child's lamp in *Sleepy Hollow*. On taking the lamp, the pedestal becomes an animated mouth and the walls come alive with glowing red eyes. When he finally realises the Mage's treachery Aladdin mopes around, trapped in the cave, chin on hands like a depressed Rodin's Thinker gazing upon a similarly-posed skeleton. Another Burton trend comes through the Sultan's love of gadgetry. When challenged to come up with the best gadget ever, in return for his daughter's hand, the resourceful genie-aided hero devises the inspired solution of a small box that acts like a window on the world. Even in a fantastical mythical past Burton has managed to include a television - a gadget that later proves a handy cell for the deviant Moroccan, doomed to be forever prodded with red forks by devils for the Sultan's entertainment.

Nimoy is great as the long-bearded wizened baddy, Joseph Maher's Sultan is marvellously vacant (and content with being regularly massaged by four green arms protruding from his throne) but the real star is James Earl Jones as the twin genies of Ring and Lamp. Always appearing in a billow of blue glitter and smoke, the pointy-eared blue Genie of the Lamp alternates (often midsentence) between horrible threats of violence and ingratiating smarm - an Arabian Nights version of Betelgeuse with a bellowing laugh of sheer insanity. The younger performers cannot match these fanciful characters but that's down to the nature of the hero and heroine to be blander than their larger-than-life counterparts.

Tim Burton for pre-teens (get 'em hooked while they're young), *Aladdin* is at best a minor work, but is entertaining and sows plenty of seeds for future projects.

The Verdict: 3/5

Look Bike In Anger

"Hello girls and boys, And welcome to my toys."

Pee-wee's Playhouse

With a couple of fine shorts and some TV work behind him, Burton had clearly shown his unusual talent to the world, but was still awaiting his first foray into the fabulous world of feature films. It came about quite by chance. Pee-wee Herman was a character created by Paul Reubens, a member of the Groundlings troupe of comedians. Pee-wee had become a surprise hit on a TV special and Warner Brothers were keen to bring the character to life on the big screen, but Reubens had been having trouble finding a suitable director. So he went to a party (as you do) and asked if anyone knew of someone available. One guest mentioned *Frankenweenie* and recommended it to Reubens noting Shelley Duvall's involvement. Shelley, a friend, enthused about it and its young director, and arranged for Reubens to see a screening the very next day. He knew instantly that Burton was the man for the job, but was told that he probably wouldn't be interested. Still he sent Burton the script, and the pair hit it off almost immediately.

Pee-wee's Big Adventure (1985)

Crew: Dir: Tim Burton, Prd: Richard Gilbert Abramson, Robert Shapiro, Scr: Paul Reubens, Phil Hartman, Michael Varhol, DP: Victor J Kemper, Music: Danny Elfman, 87 mins

Cast: Paul Reubens (Pee-wee Herman), Elizabeth Daily (Dottie), Mark Holton (Francis), Diane Salinger (Simone), Monte Landis (Mario), James Brolin (PW), Morgan Fairchild ("Dottie"), Dee Snider (himself)

Plot: Pee-wee Herman, child in a man's body, lives in his house in the heart of suburban America. Packed with all the latest lifestyle-enhancing gadgets, things are idyllic in Pee-wee's world. His companion Speck has his own interior doghouse with his name emblazoned in neon letters above the entrance. This in itself would make for a contented life but there's more to come, for the bestest toy a boy could have resides in the heavily secured secret garage in his garden. It's red and white. It's sleek. It has more secret functions than James Bond's latest car. It is Pee-wee's super-duper bike - quite possibly the fabbest thing in the whole wide world and coveted by rich-kid rival Francis. The icing on the cake is that Pee-wee's long suffering admirer, the aptly named Dottie, conveniently works in Chuck's Bike-O-Rama, so that Pee-wee can get the latest gizmos and accessories the millisecond they become available. However, nirvana can be a brittle thing, poised precariously on the edge of the chasm of despair. And so it proves for Pee-wee when a disaster of cata-clysmic proportions strikes. His bike is stolen. Running the whole gamut of emotions from anguish to despair, seething rage to melancholia, he tries everything to find it. He organises re-enactments of the crime, runs an exten-sive poster campaign offering fabulous wealth for the finder, goes on radio chat shows and even confronts his rotund nemesis, currently engaged in bath-time Godzilla dramatics. Finally, he is reduced to seeking the esoteric help of Madame Ruby, a fortune-teller who reveals that his precious pedalling push-bike is to be found in the basement of the Alamo. In fact, the bike had been bought by devious Francis, who employed a local thug to purloin it for his own nefarious purposes, but shied away from the stolen goods when the heat was on. It is now on a journey of its own...

Pee-wee meanwhile decides to hitch-hike to Texas in double-quick time. He is first picked up by an escaped convict, then involved in a car crash and gets a lift from a scary dead lorry driver called Large Marge. Following a spell watching the sunrise with dreaming waitress Simone inside a model dinosaur, he escapes a sound beating from Simone's insanely jealous boyfriend Andy before catching a train to the Alamo with a singing hobo. Imagine the pain and desperation when he realises that the Alamo has no basement and the vested powers of clairvoyance possessed by the fortune-teller were dubious to say the least. Matters take a turn for the bizarre as an enraged Andy forces Pee-wee to become one of the finest rodeo riders in the West. Fleeing further mishap, it's a case of out of the frying pan and into the fire as he riles some Hell's Angels by accidentally trashing their bikes. Fortunately, a combination of gutsy dancing skills and an opportunity to describe his own bike-centred woes endears him to them and they loan him a motorbike. Sadly Pee-wee's bike skills are more adept when it comes to pedalling and he ends up in hospi-tal following a disastrous accident. As luck would have it, this spell reveals the awful truth about his beloved bike - it is to be given away as a gift to a pre-cocious and bad tempered child superstar on the set of his latest Warner Brothers' comedy. But surely Pee-wee wouldn't stoop as low as to stealing back his bike from the hands of a little boy? Have you been paying attention? Of course he would, he's Pee-me-me-me-wee Herman. What would he care about some snivelling rich kid's feelings? The question is not would he do it, but can he get away with it? Well one thing's for sure, it's a very big adven-ture and would make a smashing movie.

Comment: The secret word is: aggravating.

Tim Burton's first feature is a non-stop roller-coaster comedy filled to the brim with visual ideas, action set pieces and an almost stream-of-conscious-ness approach to matters that feels closer to the work of the silent comedians or Hong Kong comedies. By mixing slapstick with surrealism the results are exhilarating and occasionally exhausting. Whether or not you actually find it

24

funny (comedy is after all a very personal thing) lies on the shoulders of one man: Pee-wee Herman. Pee-wee's comic persona is so ingrained that he is billed as playing himself and not a role for Reubens. The combination of an ill-fitting suit (a stalwart comedy device), pasty face make-up, lipstick and rouged cheeks gives the general countenance of a silent comedian and certainly his physical exaggerations are expressionist rather than realistic. The difference lies in the term silent - Pee-wee isn't. Whether Pee-wee's irritating giggles and brat-like demeanour ("I know you are, but what am I?") bring you tears of laughter or tears of rage are purely a matter of taste.

Pee-wee's house may well have gestated as an extension of his Playhouse world but it is filled with resolutely Burtonesque imagery and gadgets with a plethora of skeletons, dinosaurs and pumpkins. When Pee-wee announces "Let's have breakfast," the house whirls into action as machines prepare and serve his food. These aren't boring toasters and microwaves but Heath Robinson style contraptions that are as much about being machines as having a purpose. In *Edward Scissorhands*, these devices would be streamlined into the charming cookie-makers but here they are far more chaotic. His toast is carried by a Pterodactyl skeleton, eggs cracked by a nodding bird, his orange juice freshly squeezed in the jaws of a tyrannosaurus as he slides down his fireman's pole to enjoy the food. "Hello Mr breakfast!" The cutlery he uses is oversized, further emphasising that he lives in a perpetual child's world, and cleaning his teeth is just an excuse to pretend to be rabid. "Mad dog!" Strangely, despite his childishness, there are no parental figures or authorities to curtail the extravagance. The only counselling he receives in the morning comes from a gadget advising that he should "not leave the house today," which he promptly ignores. Everyone takes him for granted as though there is nothing unusual going on.

Loosely this is a skewed retelling of Vittorio De Sica's classic *Bicycle Thieves* (1948) but treated as a comedy. (This approach was also favoured by Maurizio Nichetti's *The Icicle Thief* (1989).) Indeed, the earnestness with which Pee-wee demands the return of his bike reaches the fevered pitch of De Sica's subtle melodrama, but there is a fundamental difference: Pee-wee's need of the bike is purely self-centred. He will not starve if it never returns and remains a spoilt child wailing for his lost toy. In fact the one thing that makes *Pee-wee's Big Adventure* such a difficult film to watch for those that can't take to Pee-wee is precisely this: he is a deeply unsympathetic character whose only thoughts are for his own well-being, without an ounce of respect for anything else. That his arch-rival Francis is more loathsome does not excuse Pee-wee's behaviour. When Pee-wee discovers his bike is at the Alamo, he heads straight there. He doesn't bother to ensure that Speck is being cared for (fortunately Dottie had the forethought to look after him, canine watchers) and his treatment of his girlfriend is appalling. The only thing she really wants to do is go to a quiet drive-in with him but he will have none of it. Even when he declares over the phone, "I've learnt something out on the road here Dottie – humility," he swiftly fakes a crackly line when she suggests going to the movies. That she finally gets her wish is only because the film they go to see is all about him. How telling. And yet, despite this completely self-obsessed attitude everyone around him seems to love him. His only genuine rivals come in the shape of two children (Francis and the deeply obnoxious Kevin) and Andy, whose mental faculties place him not far from childhood.

Regardless of the appeal of Pee-wee himself, there is still a lot to enjoy. The road movie structure is mixed with surrealist slapstick in the mould of the absurd film *Hellzapoppin'* (1941) or the extended chase sequences of Buster Keaton and Keystone Cops films. The major set piece towards the film's close consolidates these themes - it is a chase, it's surreal and reflects the process of making a film. Pee-wee has finally discovered his bike and sets about reclaiming it by donning a nun's costume on the set of the latest wholesome feelgood comedy starring child brat Kevin Morton. Seizing his opportunity, he makes his escape, but is swiftly pursued through the studio lots, picking up a bizarre entourage of extras, actors and props along the way. He passes twin elephants (one magenta, one cyan), is followed by studio golf carts, bursts onto the set of a cheesy beach movie and enters the spirit of Christmas at the North Pole. He then gets to trash Tokyo along with Godzilla and Ghidorah before improving, sorry ruining, a Twisted Sister video and leaping Tarzan-style across a lake on a vine. During this escalating sequence of mayhem he gets to show off his remarkable array of Bond-like gadgets attached to the bike. The scene is exhilarating and seemingly endless, but the original cut was longer, even finding time to put in a Sergio Leone western!

The finest moments of the film occur whenever there are dreams because these provide the most arresting imagery. They also link into Pee-wee's mindset so that on occasion we literally see his view of the world. To get in touch with his surreal and offbeat world, the film even begins with a dream - Pee-wee winning the Tour de France, his frantic pedalling outdistancing the professionals with ease. Later on, bikes appear in his waking dreams as he is tormented following the loss of his own. Waiting near its last known resting place, he watches despondently as, in his mind, everyone has a bike apart from him - unicycles, penny farthings, tandems and even a little electric one torture his delusions. His final bike dream takes this delirium to its logical conclusion. Stuck in hospital and despairing of ever seeing his bike again, he has gone from the optimism of his Tour de France dream into a deranged Boschlike circus Hell: ambulance clowns cart away his bike, wheeling it to an operating theatre for surgery before sending the metallic wreck straight to the burning furnaces of Hell. These sequences are lit like a stage show with some wonderful use of forced perspective chequered sets that work as prototypes for similar ones in *Beetlejuice* and *Sleepy Hollow*.

Style And Score: For the music Burton turned to Danny Elfman, whose score is completely in tune with the mad circus style events being portrayed and goes some way to explain why many have compared the film to, of all things, *Fellini Satyricon* (1969) and *8½* (1963)! Elfman would also be responsible for the theme music to *Pee-wee's Playhouse* as well as the (decidedly inferior) sequel *Big Top Pee-wee* (1988). The score is used not just as incidental or background music but becomes part of the film itself. When Pee-wee confronts Francis, the knock on his mansion door is accentuated precisely within the score. Visually the film is bright, garish and bold. The attention lavished on Pee-wee's bike when it's first revealed is similar not only to the unveiling of the Batmobile but also the worship of the bike shown in Kenneth Anger's influential underground film *Scorpio Rising* (1964), even down to the coloured lighting and dissection of the bike's form.

Making Of: The budget, while not minuscule, was certainly tight for the freewheeling scope of the film. A lot of the props were actually Reubens' (including most of the bathroom set) and some Burton's, but were mainly procured from thrift shops. For the bike-riding scenes Reubens was dragged along the back of a truck but still had to maintain frantic peddling or risk injury. The episodic nature of the film and the tight shooting schedule meant that each scene, with the exception of the studio chase, had about a day's worth of set-ups. The truck stop where Pee-wee meets Simone is a real place, complete with dinosaur park and bar.

Playground: Actor Paul Reubens developed the character Pee-wee Herman in the late 1970s and used him in a stand-up comedy routine steeped in innuendo and double entendre. (Some suggestive dialogue remains in the film - "So is my horn ready yet?" he asks Dottie.) The combination of surrealism, childishness and crude gags made for cult viewing. *The Pee-wee Herman Show*, ran for five months at the Roxy Club in LA and was broadcast as a HBO special. Pee-wee became a regular talk show attendee and frequent live performer. He put aside the more adult material of his shows following the surprise success of *Pee-wee's Big Adventure,* and transferred them to children's television in 1986. Freed of the inhibitions of being an adult, the perpetually childlike Pee-wee was wild, free of consequence from any action and lived in a Day-Glo playhouse full of strange creatures and cool toys. The show succeeded because it used childish language, full of secret codes, clubs and petty repetition ("Didn't"/"Did") but crucially *Pee-wee's Playhouse* didn't alienate the adult viewers. The show ran for five successful years. However, Pee-wee's demise was swift due to an unfortunate incident at a cinema of dubious repute in 1991. Burton gave Reubens a cameo in *Batman Returns* (as well as a character voice on *The Nightmare Before Christmas*) and he has since returned to the public gaze in such films as the atrocious *Buffy The Vampire Slayer* (1992), Danny de Vito's excellent *Matilda* (1996) and the underrated comedy *Mystery Men* (1999).

Trivia: Who do you think is in the waving clown costume outside Mario's? None other than Tim Burton. The female biker - "Why don't you let me have him first?" - was in fact Elvira, another Groundling. Originally there were supposed to be three coloured elephants, but the yellow one got stuck in transit on the Mona freeway and shooting had to continue without it. Reubens required a shoe polisher who followed him on hands and knees to ensure that his shoes stayed white and shiny for every shot. Not only did they get permission to use Godzilla in the film they even used some of the original sound effects too. Reubens had a hatred of snakes but Burton told him that "I can't make it work with fake snakes" on the morning they shot the burning pet shop scene. The resulting reaction was real.

Madame Ruby Predicts: The establishing shot of the studio prior to the climactic chase features the original Batmobile.

The Verdict: 3/5 (5/5 if you can stomach Pee-wee)

It's Showtime!

Pee-wee's Big Adventure was well received but it meant that Burton was perceived as a guy who made quirky low-key comedies. He wanted to direct another feature, but none of the offers that came his way seemed quite right. So he returned to TV.

The Jar (1985)

Crew: Dir: Tim Burton, Scr: Michael McDowell, Larry Wilson from the story by Ray Bradbury, Music: Danny Elfman with Steve Bartek, 24 mins

Cast: Griffin Dunne (Noel), Fiona Lewis (Erica), Paul Bartel (Art Critic), Laraine Newman (Periwinkle)

Plot: Art, that strange and terrifying entity which only seems to appreciate you when you are dead. Noel is determined not to let fame creep up on him posthumously, but is not having much success. That is until he comes across a jar whose contents fascinate anyone who gazes upon it. Passing it off as his own he becomes the darling of the art circuit, but at a price. Success breeds contempt resulting in tension between himself and his wife Erica, whose extramarital dalliances and jealous demeanour lead to a spiteful plan to remove the source of her husband's celebrity. But what exactly is in the jar?

Comment: Burton directed *The Jar* for an episode of the revitalised *Alfred Hitchcock Presents* series. The original series started in 1955 and ran for ten years, covering a staggering 266 episodes (plus another 93 for *The Alfred Hitchcock Hour*), and was resurrected during the 1980s for a modern audience. The original productions were bookended by the master of suspense telling amusing macabre anecdotes and these would be reused (albeit colourised) for the remakes. The original version of *The Jar* was directed by Norman Lloyd and first aired on television in February 1964, for *The Alfred Hitchcock Hour*. Scripted by James Bridges from a short story by the great Ray Bradbury, it follows the themes we have come to know from Bradbury's work: small-town America; carnivals; the delight in revealing the dark depths underneath the surface of society; and dire consequences. Sadly, Bradbury's combination of innocent nostalgia and blind psychosis is a difficult balance to produce in any medium – his work has a fragile nastiness that should, but doesn't, translate well to the screen.

Paul Bartel makes a welcome appearance here, his second in a Burton production, and does much to liven up the proceedings. But the irrelevant Nazi connections and liberties with the story take its toll over the acting and the unusual effects. In the end this is a reasonable television production with all the inherent failings of the medium and is not as poor as Burton himself remembers it. At least the twist in the tale remains and it's suitably creepy.

The Score: "One of my few excursions into TV scoring, and my favourite," Danny Elfman, *Music For A Darkened Theatre Vol 1*. What starts out as a pure Elfman score (albeit with a reduced number of musicians) soon becomes a wonderful take on Bernard Herrmann as themes from classic Hitchcock films are blended together seamlessly, to produce something that is at once homage and also an in-joke on the theme of the series.

The Verdict: 3/5

Beetlejuice came Burton's way via David Geffen and he immediately took it on board. In a spooky case of coincidence, the story was created by Michael McDowell and Larry Wilson who had written Burton's *The Jar*. Burton assembled previous collaborators, all of whom helped give the film that essential quirkiness: Thomas Ackerman had shot *Frankenweenie*, Rick Heinrichs helped design the film and Danny Elfman provided the score.

Beetlejuice (1988)

Crew: Dir: Tim Burton, Prd: Michael Bender, Richard Hashimoto, Larry Wilson, Scr: Michael McDowell, Warren Skaaren, Story: Michael McDowell, Larry Wilson, DP: Thomas E Ackerman, Music: Danny Elfman, 88 mins

Cast: Alec Baldwin (Adam Maitland), Geena Davis (Barbara Maitland), Annie McEnroe (Jane), Maurice Page (Ernie), Michael Keaton (Betelgeuse), Winona Ryder (Lydia), Catherine O'Hara (Delia Deetz), Jeffrey Jones (Charles Deetz)

Plot: The Maitlands are a happily married couple with no children, no pets and no worries. They have a beautiful house on top of a hill and, while Adam spends his day making wonderfully intricate model towns, Barbara makes sure the house is clean, tidy and wholesomely homely. So what if it's a bit twee and saccharine, they like it that way. Naturally, such a scene of domestic bliss would make for pretty dull viewing so, in the name of dramatic storytelling, it becomes necessary for the Maitlands to face some apparently insurmountable obstacle in order to facilitate a more interesting cinematic experience. And sure enough such an obstacle rears its ugly head, for their nagging friend Jane sells their house to the Deetz family, a thoroughly ghastly nouveau-riche couple with a misanthropic and long-suffering daughter Lydia. But it seems that the Maitlands can do nothing about their unwanted visitors, nay homeowners, because they are dead. Following a car accident involving a dog on a bridge they find themselves in the afterlife, forced to remain inside their house as the realm beyond the front door is a barren desert of desolation populated by giant, vicious sand worms intent on masticating upon any passing ghost. Not pleasant. Help (of a kind) is available in the shape of *The*

Handbook For The Recently Deceased, a handy tome given out to all newly-deads to aid them in those troublesome early centuries. Armed with their new-found knowledge, they find their way to a bizarre bureaucratic world and discover to their horror (thanks to caseworker Juno) that they are doomed to haunt their property for a long, long time.

Drastic events call for drastic measures. The Deetz family are intent on destroying everything the Maitlands hold dear with the help of Otho, an interior designer whose designs are, how shall we say, radical. For the time being, all they have is their attic room in which to hatch a plan. What do ghosts do for a living? They haunt! They construct all kinds of macabre scenarios for the Deetz family but yet again are foiled as they cannot be seen except by Lydia who is at least sympathetic to their cause. They may be forced to live in a dark room but, as she points out, with parents like hers, "My whole life is a dark room." The situation is intolerable. But then they come across an advert for Betelgeuse, a bio-exorcist, satisfaction guaranteed (with minor exceptions). Despite the imploring pleas of every dead person they've met, they summon him by calling his name three times. Now they have a professional, albeit a manic one who's also an opportunist lecher, and he gets straight to work. Sadly his first attempt, possessing a dinner party and getting the food to attack the guests, ends in disaster as the Deetz family find the concept of a haunted house a sure-fire way to become the darlings of their social circuit. Tragic times for our once-happy couple. Not only do they have to contend with their house being abused by an unwelcome family, they have also unleashed a chaotic and insane phantasmagorical force of a magnitude hitherto unimagined.

Comment: Beetlejuice, although only a second feature, laid the groundwork for the rest of Burton's career by becoming a surprise hit. Its budget was a mid-range $13 million (by no means a large amount for such an effects-heavy film), but Burton made the most of what he was given. Despite *Beetlejuice* generally remaining in a budget-friendly single location, the Maitlands' house, it manages to branch out into the most absurd fantasy places. The purgatory sequences in particular have very little basis in real-world logic and provide us with a plethora of strange characters, all apparently victims of violent death. There's the man who fell asleep with a lit cigarette, a magician's assistant (she may be in pieces but can still respond if someone gets fresh with her) and the amazing shrunken-head man (whose condition's cause is only revealed at the film's close). All are overseen by an officious secretary and a numbered ticket system just like the ones they have at supermarket deli counters, only worse. Heaven isn't short of civil servants, clerks and councillors. It's all very *Brazil* (1985).

Michael Keaton tackles his part with aplomb. Twitching around like someone not entirely in control of his mental faculties, he crouches until ready to spring in a burst of manic energy. When first summoned he erupts into the Maitlands' existence like a cross between an electrocuted cadaver and Tigger from *Winnie The Pooh*. He jabbers like Robin Williams in *Aladdin* and alters his pace like the Martian Spy Girl in *Mars Attacks!* He is not only a sexist pig he is also incredibly rude to those who are ultimately his (unwitting) rescuers. When he is first released into the Maitlands' attic he takes one look at the model village that has been his Astroturfed prison, comments "Nice fuckin' model" and makes, how shall we put it, a masturbatory gesture to Adam. He is besotted with Lydia (as he is with all women), and the only way they can stop him is by Juno shrinking him back to model size and shoving him in a whore-house. Betelgeuse's TV advert is a quick-fire low-budget affair. The hard sell and the cheesy graphics coupled with Betelgeuse's infectious "say it once, say it twice, third time's a charm" delivery is pure American kitsch. It's an energetic role which, on first viewing, can be a little hard to take. Keaton's ability as a comedy performer has been used to great effect in such films as Ron Howard's black comedy *Night Shift* (1982) and a remarkable turn in Kenneth Branagh's *Much Ado About Nothing* (1993) but sadly has failed to turn him into a truly A-list actor. This is a pity because on the basis of his performances he's a versatile actor and *Beetlejuice* showed just how far he could go. In contrast, the Maitlands are subdued, but this is the point - they are a happy middle-class family thrown into a world of turmoil. The contrast between meek and manic has been held as a criticism of the film but is really what makes it work so well. When they try to scare the Deetz family the results may be macabre (Adam hung in a closet, Barbara holding Adam's head in one hand with a gore drenched axe in the other) but they are also pitiful. They are simply not cut out to be as ruthless as Betelgeuse or the Deetz family.

Lydia is, in her own words, "strange and unusual" for, as Adam points out, "If I'd seen a ghost at your age I'd have been scared out of my wits." Rather like the President's daughter in *Mars Attacks!* she is the intelligent insular daughter in a rich family. She befriends the Maitlands and despite her misanthropic nature remains loyal to them, standing up to Betelgeuse with some courage and wisely refusing to say his name three times... initially. In the end, Lydia does capitulate to Betelgeuse's advances and agrees to marry him, but only in return for his help when the Maitlands are drained of their existence for their refusal to be party ghosts. Having agreed to matrimony, Betelgeuse exerts his own brand of chaos once more. With Adam and Barbara still recovering from their ordeal, Lydia awaits her fate in front of the officiating priest, a giant bug thing who is careful about saying "the B word." Of course it all ends out happily enough with Lydia becoming an 'A' grade student for her adopted dead parents and Betelgeuse getting his come-uppance. Lydia even manages to do a Mary Poppins impersonation with an awestruck team of dead American football players. What more could a young girl want?

Otho is like a rumbustious Pee-wee but far more damaging. His clothing, a casual suit with bright red shoes, mirrors Pee-wee's but his intentions are decidedly suspect. He uses the Maitlands' handbook to manipulate them for his own nefarious purposes. "I know just as much about the supernatural as I do about interior design," he reveals and he's right. In many ways he is the villain of the piece rather than the psychotic Betelgeuse. He hasn't got the excuse of centuries of festering insanity. His purpose is purely capitalist in motivation.

The film constantly refers to B-movie and horror film conventions, despite being a comedy. The expressionism inherent in the afterlife corridors features forced perspectives of the kind immortalised in Robert Wiene's classic *The Cabinet Of Dr Caligari*. The symbol of the haunted house atop a hill is a common one and a staple of the genre. The house is akin to *The House On Haunted Hill* (1958), a William Castle film featuring Vincent Price. It is not the only Price film that is referred to. Prior to being summoned, Betelgeuse lived in Adam's model town. Luring a fly with a big bar of candy he eats the unfortunate insect who, prior to its digestion, manages to squeak out "Help me," mirroring the shock ending of *The Fly* (1958). The title sequence too plays with the conventions of the horror film with its helicopter shot (*The Shining* (1980), another haunted house flick) swooping over the countryside, blending into Adam's model town before focusing on the model house. Crawling over the house is a huge spider recalling the mutant insect subgenre of horror films (*Giant Spider Invasion* (1975), *Them!* (1954), *Empire Of The Ants* (1977)). What sets *Beetlejuice* apart from being just a homage is the way it plays with conventions and expectations about the genre. Usually a haunted house film has the humans being haunted by ghosts, not the other way round.

Style And Score: The repeated aural motif is that of 'Day-O' and other calypso numbers. This helps give an otherworldly feel because, along with the house and costumes, it is difficult to place the film in time. We know it is 'sort of' contemporary, but the use of such archaic recordings places events any-when. Similarly, Danny Elfman's score is an unusual driving "Oom-pah" sound that is reminiscent in tempo to his theme music for *The Simpsons*, further emphasising some of the more cartoon aspects of the film.

The design is inherently Burton, and many of the ideas that made it onto the screen came from his own sketches. He devised Lydia's gothic countenance, how Adam and Barbara should transform themselves in horrifying ways and how some of the deceased lost their lives. When Betelgeuse is finally unleashed he becomes an entire horror fairground with merry-go-round hat, bat ears and 'test your strength' hammers on the end of his stripy arms. To the Maitlands, outside the wholesome house is a barren Daliesque desert landscape with howling winds and *Dune* style sand worms that roam the plains. These are huge stripy beasts with further copies of themselves emerging from their jaws. They resemble the present-eating snake from *The Nightmare Before Christmas* and are animated using stop-motion.

Making Of: Only $1 million was set aside to realise the special effects work, a combination of in-camera effects, model work, stop-frame animation and extensive prosthetics. This budgetary restriction worked in the film's favour - it looks so quaint and organic. The film is not terribly well closed and the ending was in doubt even after photography had finished. The conclusion finally used came about as the result of audience testing and for want of anything better!

Trivia: During the course of one of his many mad turns, pasty-faced poltergeist Betelgeuse transforms his own head into a miniature merry-go-round. Crowning this delightful ensemble is the familiar head of Jack Skellington. Burton's original choice for the role of Betelgeuse was Sammy Davies Jr. but this was turned down by the studios. It was Geffen who suggested Keaton. Warner Brothers originally wanted the film to be entitled *House Ghosts*, but both that and Burton's mocking compromise suggestion *Scared Sheetless* were mercifully dropped in favour of the original title. *Beetlejuice* won an Oscar for best make-up.

The Afterlife: Considering its budget and the initially low-key publicity surrounding the film, *Beetlejuice* went on to perform excellent trade. Its surprise success, considering it featured no A-list actors and a director still wet behind the ears, led to Burton's rapid rise up the Hollywood ranks. Despite not having much tie-in merchandise on its release (it was not expected to be big) you could subsequently buy all manner of toys and even sweets connected with *Beetlejuice*. This was mainly because the success of the film led to a spin-off cartoon series. It was produced by Burton but did not feature the voices of any of those connected with the film and despite its target audience being children, managed to sneak a fair amount of adult material into the living room. As is the way with cartoons, those adults that would be offended by their content dismiss them as childish and don't watch them anyway. Altering the formula, Betelgeuse has now become a chum to a substantially younger Lydia. The standard 22-minute format saw the programme chalk up four seasons. So in many ways it was two successes for the price of one and despite its low-key entrance, the character of Betelgeuse has lasted well beyond the confines of his feature film.

The Verdict: 4/5

Holy Budgets, Batman

Burton had been mooted as a possible director for *Batman* prior to his second feature, but the financial success of *Beetlejuice* meant that his involvement was in no doubt. Despite being a kind of fiftieth birthday celebration for the caped crusader, the gestation period for the film had been a long time in coming. Benjamin Melniker and Michael Uslan had bought the rights to use DC's character in 1979. Peter Guber became involved and they had to decide who would take the director's chair. This happened over several years as Guber changed studios, eventually finding himself at Warner Brothers. Several other directors (including Ivan *Ghostbusters* Reitman and Joe *Gremlins* Dante) had been attached to the project before Burton finally took it on. Despite production problems, tight deadlines, an incomplete script, rewrites and a budget that spiralled way past its original (already substantial) forecast, *Batman* was an unqualified commercial hit, becoming the first film to net $100,000,000 in its first ten days. If that was not enough, Burton had even managed to find time to fall in love and marry German artist Lena Gieseke on February 24, 1989. Suddenly Burton was big. Seemingly from nowhere this fragile-looking, shaggy-haired kid had produced, at that time, one of the highest grossing films ever. He was 30 years old.

Batman (1989)

Crew: Dir: Tim Burton, Prd: Jon Peters, Peter Guber, Co-Prd: Chris Kenny, Exec Prd: Benjamin Melniker, Michael Uslan, Scr: Sam Hamm, Warren Skaaren, DP: Roger Pratt, Music: Danny Elfman, 121 mins

Cast: Jack Nicholson (Jack Napier/The Joker), Michael Keaton (Bruce Wayne/Batman), Kim Basinger (Vicki Vale), Jack Palance (Carl Grissom), Robert Wuhl (Alexander Knox), Billy Dee Williams (Harvey Dent), Pat Hingle (Commissioner Gordon), Jerry Hall (Alicia), Michael Gough (Alfred)

"The words Gotham City are synonymous with crime"

Plot: Gotham City, a sprawling metropolis on the dawn of its 200th anniversary. Celebrations are planned but it's hard to work up any enthusiasm when the economy is failing and the balloons haven't even been ordered. It's a tough call for District Attorney Harvey Dent and Mayor Borg. Compounding the malaise is Gotham's rampant crime wave - a virulent spread of illegal activity that casts its insidious tentacles wide into the community. Even the police force are in the pockets of the crime barons, particularly slimeball backhander Eckhardt. Chief cause of the escalating chaos is Carl Grissom, but not for long. What can halt the tidal wave of fear and oppression? In the underworld tales are told in half whispers of an indestructible vigilante who bursts from the shadows to administer on-the-spot justice to wrongdoers - the Bat. "They say he can't be killed. They say he drinks blood." But is the Bat for real? And if so, is replacing one form of illegal activity with another a viable solution to the city's problems? That's the question reporter Knox is keen to discover despite ridicule from his sceptical colleagues. He does have an ally in the shapely shape of top photographer Vicki Vale and they are determined to ferret out the truth.

But who is the mysterious Batman (as he likes to be called) and what's his gripe with the criminal fraternity? He is Bruce Wayne, millionaire eccentric who conducts his own brand of clandestine legal enforcement from the technologically-enhanced depths of Wayne Mansion. Aided and abetted by family butler Alfred, he is still deeply traumatised by the savage execution of his parents in a Gotham alley when he was a child. Riddled with angst and driven to the shadows despite his outward show of business savvy and opulence, he still seeks the killer. That killer is the morally redundant Jack Napier, a dandified hoodlum who works partly as Grissom's left-hand man. Thing is, Grissom realises Napier's potential to usurp his position as potentate of pernicious perpetration and arranges to have the upstart surreptitiously removed by Eckhardt and his boys in blue in a stitch-up job at Axis chemicals. Bruce Wayne hears about the potential hassles at Axis during a fund-raising party, makes his excuses, dons cape and flies to the scene of unrest. The resulting showdown between good cops, bad cops, villains and Batman ends in a mess with Jack apparently falling to his doom in a vat of highly toxic waste. Would that it were that simple. Jack's resurrection from the bubbling cauldron of noxious liquid results in bleached skin, green hair, a mind warped beyond recognition and an unnaturally wide grin plastered across his face. He has become The Joker, a new breed of supervillain.

The Joker quickly takes his place as the head of Gotham City, eliminating Grissom and anyone else who dares get in his way. He has, however, a more hands-on approach to chaos than his predecessor, preferring to view his unifying vision as art rather than crime. Alicia, his long-suffering girlfriend, has her face tastefully remodelled to his exacting standards before she drops in his estimation and elevation, sadly falling from a tall building. The Joker's new object of affection is none other than Vicki Vale, the snag being that Vicki is currently bedding Bruce Wayne. The Joker's masterplan is on a far grander and more sinister scale than pinching Batman's girlfriend though. Under the guise of philanthropy he intends to revitalise the city's flagging celebrations by distributing $20 million in hard cash to the gathered citizens of Gotham. This is, of course, a front for a heinous plan that would see the populace succumb to poison gas at the very moment of financially induced euphoria. The effects of the deadly substance are already known as the Joker has been experimenting with concoctions introduced into cosmetic products which causes the victims to die laughing, a grotesque smile permanently etched on their visage as rigor mortis sets in. Only one person is capable and rich enough to deal with such a catastrophic occurrence... the Dark Knight... Batman. But his concerns are of a personal nature too, for the devious Joker has kidnapped the volatile and vivacious Vicki Vale and his intentions for her seem less savoury than merely waltzing atop the bell tower of Gotham Cathedral...

Comment: Of all his films *Batman* somehow feels the least Tim Burton despite sticking to the themes and ideas that run through the rest of his work. Visually the film is undeniably his, but it appears occasionally at odds with the demands of a commercial blockbuster. Make no mistake *Batman* was, and is, an event movie. The buzz about the film, the hype and the long marketing strategy suggested it would be popular, but its success was never guaranteed. Warner Brothers took an incredible risk placing such a relatively inexperienced young director on such a high-profile movie. Indeed, their very future could have been at stake if the project failed to ignite the box office. Of course, we now know that this is Burton's most financially successful film. (At the time of writing, *Planet Of The Apes* is doing big business.) In return for being entrusted with such a prestige project, Burton played by the rules and didn't over-indulge on the personal visions. The rewards for this approach turned out to be A-List status and far greater artistic freedom in the future - a price well worth paying. The most obvious departure from his first two features lies in the pacing and structure of the overall script. While *Pee-wee* and *Beetlejuice* are self-contained, narratively closed films, they are organic and undisciplined in structure, almost stream-of-consciousness film-making brimming with ideas, which forms part of their charm. *Batman* is in the more classically rigid Hollywood mould - the three-act story. Later Burton films would certainly be more disciplined than his first two but would never return to the restrictive rigor shown here. Act One (30 minutes) establishes the setting and ends with a great plot change - the birth of the Joker. Act Two (60 minutes) sees the rise of the Joker and escalation of his plans counterpointed by developing character relationships. Act Three (30 minutes) is denouement and resolution. Having been shown the Joker's plan, it's now down to Batman to set things right. These acts occur so punctually you can set your clock by them.

Much criticism was made of Burton's insistence on Michael Keaton in the role of Batman and that the role is bland compared with Jack Nicholson's Joker. In some respects Batman is overshadowed by the Joker. The structure favours the Joker's story arc and he is a substantially more flamboyant individual. But this is the point. To have two insane costumed hyperactive characters would have made for far less focused viewing, Batman needs to be calm and rational to be credible as the force of good. To make him manic would fuel the insinuation that he is as bad as the criminals. Not that Batman is without humour. Certainly, in his guise as Bruce Wayne there are a number of opportunities for Keaton to display a subtly comic talent. But ultimately Bruce Wayne needs to become Batman to deny his responsibilities and to pay for his inability to prevent his parents' death. Once he dons the costume he is freed of the burden of his financial status and also his melancholia. Both the Joker and Batman are of the same cut - the implication is that the Joker has grown up alone too, the difference between them makes the film reactionary. Money determines their morality no matter how much donning a mask equalises their class status. This explains the Joker's attack on the art world as reacting against the bourgeoisie - he vandalises the classics (except a Francis Bacon!) because he seeks to become what he hates and what he isn't. They may both hide behind masks but Batman's is of his choosing and upbringing - he is like Zorro, a proud aristocrat fighting for the populace. Another difference in family status between the two opposites is in the treatment of the surrogate father figure. In the Joker's case, Grissom is the stern face of fatherly authority who realises the danger of Jack's ambition and attempts to execute him. The Joker retaliates by killing his surrogate father. Freed of the burden of parental control he becomes dangerously childlike. Batman, on the other hand, has the responsible, caring surrogate in the shape of Alfred, who looks after the spoilt little rich kid. In many ways *Batman* is a rallying cry for responsible parenting...

When Bruce Wayne becomes Batman he changes psychologically to match his image. It is hard to imagine Wayne being able to kick lowlifes through doors or perform dynamic acrobatics, but once in character he becomes that hero. The suit itself accentuates muscles. It is an external manifestation of the male ego as well as a fetish in its use of black rubber. By putting on his suit he becomes a warrior. Similarly, his vehicles are an extension of this. The Batmobile is one of the most blatant forms of onscreen penis envy committed to celluloid. Batman is clearly a man behind a mask. The Joker's attempts at public relations work because he lies about his mask. "I have just taken off my make-up. Let's see if you can take off yours" he challenges, when in fact he has used flesh-coloured paint to disguise his mutilated features. The only mask that the Joker openly shows is the one he has attached to his tragic moll Alicia (in a nod to Franju's *Les Yeux Sans Visage* (1959)), and that is to justify his warped position as "homicidal artist." While Bruce denounces the Joker's assertion that "we mustn't compare ourselves to normal people" as justification for his behaviour (very Nietzsche) he concurs in his actions - he's in denial again. He points out the similarities himself: "I made you. You made me first."

Style And Score: The loss of parents and the inability to communicate are themes of alienation inherent in Burton's work, and he uses his visual style to show this. Some of the finest moments occur not when the camera is survey-

38

ing the domineering skyline or swooping along the damp streets but in the restrictive grounds of the television set. During the scare on cosmetic products, the normally plastic-faced newscasters become dishevelled after the onscreen death of a colleague. Similarly, the Joker's fake adverts for his reign of terror are perfect precisely because they are so low-tech and ludicrous. The most obviously Burtonesque moments occur in the City's festival scene, which has a forced perspective image that only a big imagination and a bigger budget can realise. During the celebrations, the Joker plans to poison the populace by unleashing toxic gas contained within huge balloons shaped like cartoon characters. These balloons are pure Burton in their exaggerated proportions and use of striped colouring. Batman becomes the ultimate schoolboy bully when he wrenches them from the Joker using his Batwing and sets them drifting off into the stratosphere (probably causing excessive environmental damage elsewhere).

Danny Elfman's score for the film is suitably bombastic, as befits a Hollywood blockbuster. Robust and rousing it helps drive the onscreen action. Unfortunately another Summer blockbuster trend also finds its way onto the soundtrack in the shape of a number of songs by Prince. Normally tie-ins merely irritate while the closing credits are playing (e.g. *Titanic* (1998) or the otherwise flawless *Crouching Tiger, Hidden Dragon* (2000)) but instead of one music promo, Prince came up with a whole bag full and they were integrated into the narrative. The result: breaks in the film's flow, most noticeably in the art gallery scene. More annoyingly for viewers watching now, it makes the film seem dated. This last point is unforgivable as the rest of the film looks as timeless as ever, being designed to appear as a 1940s vision of the future rather than a late 1980s one. The presence of contemporary music shatters the film's 'alternative now' ethos.

Making Of: The adoption of Nicholson and the *Batman* brand name meant that this was inevitably going to be expensive. Because of the strength of the dollar at the time and the availability of large-scale studio facilities, the film was shot in the UK. Most of the stages at Pinewood were taken over to construct the huge Gotham City sets and a massive disused power station was dressed up to be the Axis Chemicals plant. Production designer Anton Furst (who had built Vietnam in London's Docklands for Stanley Kubrick's *Full Metal Jacket*) had to co-ordinate a crew of over 200 to realise the project, which also included the Batcave with its *Forbidden Planet* style matte work. Furst also designed the Batwing and the Batmobile. Virtually all of the effects work on show is of the old school variety, although the quantity of model work necessitated computer-aided camera tracking. This meant that not only did Gotham City have to be built on soundstages so that the actors could be seen walking around, it also had to be built in scaled-down form to enable the models to be shot and matched to the 'real world' version.

Batground: Bob Kane's perennial crime fighter was half a century old when Warner Brothers' film smashed onto the silver screen in 1989. Originally appearing in the pages of *Detective Comics*, stony-faced superhero The Batman, alter ego of millionaire Bruce Wayne, eventually became the subject of his own comics. He dropped the definite article from his identity and in 1940 teamed up with Robin, the Boy Wonder. Batman was a huge success and complemented DC's other major superhero Superman. Batman was always the more interesting of the two precisely because his abilities were grounded in everyday plausibility and physicality. He was human, all too human, without superpowers, x-ray eyes or extraterrestrial jiggery-pokery. His substantial fortune and will to self-improvement provided his primary advantage against his enemies. Pitted against insurmountable odds (he was even occasionally on the run from the police due to his vigilante activities) and a menagerie of bizarre and grotesque foes, Batman's success proved strong enough to branch out into the cinema in the form of two Saturday morning serials (*Batman* (1943) and *Batman And Robin* (1948)). However most people's fond recollection of the caped crusader will be of the seminal psychedelic camp excesses of the 1960s TV series (and wonderful 1966 spin-off feature) starring Adam West and Burt Ward. Despite the cult appeal of the show, it was clearly not the direction Warner Brothers wished to pursue. Their Batman needed to be more in tune with modern day sensibilities, but crucially they could not deny the film's wider distribution to a lucrative family base that would provide all-important revenue from spin-off merchandise sales. The spiralling decline in comic books, both critically and commercially, in the early part of the 1980s had been curtailed by a new breed of American comics that revitalised the market and made reading them no longer a source of embarrassment. One of these was Frank Miller's *The Dark Knight Returns* which deconstructed the Batman myth and reinvented it for a cynical age. Crime is at an all-time high and Batman's antics are questioned as fascistic and anachronistic. He is routinely patched up by Alfred for his hideous injuries and occasionally fails to save the day. This, *Batman: Year One* and *Killing Joke* provided the impetus to turn this film project into something that was more suitable for Burton's skewed view - a world of misunderstood misfits where the boundaries between good and evil are blurred. In many ways Burton's characters, and especially those that are ostensibly deemed to be villains, are the sons of Caliban - amoral, not immoral, and products of nature, not nurture.

Trivia: Taking into account only its takings at the cinema in the US (i.e. regardless of the countless amounts of merchandise sales, video rentals, sell through tapes etc.) the film earned well over $250 million. *Batman's* dark and occasionally violent content meant it was destined for a PG-13 rating in the States. In the UK this would have equated to a 15, something that Warner

Brothers were not keen on, as a lot of revenue comes from the family market (the UK rating is compulsory rather than discretionary). A new 12 rating category was introduced as a compromise. Production designer Anton Furst won an Oscar for his remarkable realisation of a truly dark Gotham City.

The Verdict: 3/5

An Uncommonly Gentle Man

> "It's in the order of their hedgerows
>
> It's in the way their curtains open and close
>
> It's in the look they give you down their nose
>
> All part of decency's jigsaw I suppose."

XTC - 'Respectable Street'

After *Batman's* enormous success Warner Brothers wanted a sequel. But Burton chose to make a personal film, based upon an image he had created many years previously. He formed a production company with Denise Di Novi and together they produced *Edward Scissorhands* for Twentieth Century-Fox.

Edward Scissorhands (1990)

Crew: Dir: Tim Burton, Prd: Denise Di Novi, Tim Burton, Ass Prd: Caroline Thompson, Exec Prd: Richard Hashimoto, Story: Tim Burton, Caroline Thompson, Scr: Caroline Thompson, DP: Stefan Czapsky, Music: Danny Elfman, 100 mins

Cast: Johnny Depp (Edward), Winona Ryder (Kim), Dianne Wiest (Peg), Vincent Price (The Inventor), Alan Arkin (Bill), Anthony Michael Hall (Jim), Kathy Baker (Joyce), O-Lan Jones (Esmerelda)

Plot: Ding dong! Avon calling. For Peg, Avon is a calling. She takes her work very seriously even if no one wants to purchase anything. Still, her entrepreneurial spirit means she is determined to increase her quota with new custom. There is one place she hasn't plied her trade and it's just at the end of the road - a mountain with a huge mansion that overlooks her neighbourhood. With some trepidation she enters the grounds and is taken aback to find that they are well tended, bright and filled with impressive topiary. Entering the foreboding mansion she comes across the shy sole resident - Edward. He has been living alone since his creator, The Inventor, passed away. What's more, Edward is not complete - instead of hands he has long razor-sharp scissors which account for the criss-cross of scars that mark his pallid face. Peg at once realises the boy is in need of help and takes him to her home. Husband Bill tries his best to understand Edward, while Peg is dedicated to finding him the right combination of Avon cosmetics and astringents to make him blend in.

The neighbourhood is buzzing about Peg's mysterious new friend and everyone wants to meet him. Edward meanwhile is coming to terms with a very different lifestyle that includes mirrors, waterbeds and trousers with braces. One thing he particularly likes is the photograph of Peg's daughter, Kim, who is currently out camping with her boyfriend Jim. Sadly their first meeting does not go entirely to plan as, returning early, Kim finds Edward in her room and is more than a touch perturbed. But Edward becomes an established part of the household and proves to be a hit with the locals... all except cranky religious organ player Esmerelda. For Edward, you see, may have trouble transferring peas from his dinner plate to his mouth but is a real artist when it comes to hedges, pets in need of fur styling and he is a coiffeur extraordinaire. A brief spell on television raises his profile and the possibility that he can get corrective surgery to become just like everyone else. But Edward is not like everyone else and, as so often happens, the fickle tastes of the general populace turn from laudation to damnation. First off, ambrosia salad supremo and bored housewife Joyce accuses poor bemused Edward of molesting her after he refuses her advances. But worse is to come. Realising that Edward will do anything for Kim and can open locked doors in a flash, Jim comes up with a plan to get rich quick. They arrange to rob Jim's tight-fisted father using Edward's impressive larceny skills but the plan is foiled and Edward is trapped inside the house, unable to get out until the police have released him in a flurry of lights, sirens and handcuffs. Released on bail he is humiliated in the eyes of the community who so recently embraced him, but does nothing to clear his name in order to protect his loved one's honour.

Christmas is approaching. The family put on a happy face despite the incredulity of their neighbours, fitting up the house in festive splendour for the approaching holidays. Edward creates an angelic ice sculpture as Bill staples fake snow onto the roof. Meanwhile Kim has realised that Jim is not the guy for her and that true love can sometimes come in the most unlikely of guises. Edward's delicate courtship and unquestioning devotion have won her over. But their worlds are far apart and the neighbours are united in their desire to see Edward ousted from the community...

Comment: For anyone captivated by *Edward Scissorhands* words are inadequate to convey the magic of the film. Ostensibly a romantic faerie tale, the whole piece works like a gothic version of *It's A Wonderful Life* (1946) for outcasts and the disenfranchised. Like Capra's originally under-appreciated favourite, *Edward Scissorhands* is a feel-good weepalong with a streak of despair about modern society running through it. One of its many triumphs is that you become aware of society's cruelties and hypocrisies without being lectured and without matters being grim. There are good people as well as bad, misguided people and people easily led and while there is internal resolution, there is no denouement for society's intrinsic problems. Capra's great trick was to leave people unaware that they were watching a cynical film and Burton follows this lead. The film is, to all intents and purposes, timeless.

There may well be colour televisions and modern day malls, but the roots lie in a 1950s/1960s past, in the neighbourhood's 'home of the future' style bungalows. This is an alternative now, the now of the faerie tale brought up to date. Bearing this in mind, the technology indicates that the bulk of the film takes place contemporaneously in 1990, which makes the actual film (told in flashback by Kim to her grandchild) set sometime around 2040, despite appearing as a mythical Victorian past.

Edward's origin is told in a series of flashbacks featuring his loving 'father' the Inventor. The death of his father is moving and shocking as he tries to use his limited emotional faculties and infant knowledge to comprehend what is happening. Edward, having no source of information about society, relies on the scant remembered advice of his creator. Thus he is a gentleman taught in matters of courtesy, but etiquette is a code that works only if embraced by all. He is placed at a severe disadvantage because of his decency. It may well be that he fails the dinner table morality test but, despite the outrage he causes in middle-class suburban society, it is they who are painfully lacking courtesy to the point of being uncouth. While his moral code is naive but internally correct, it doesn't reflect society's opinion. Like the film, Edward is a product of a bygone age, a mythical 'better time' when people cared for the pleasantries of polite society and not the greed of the modern consumer. Morally, Edward was brought up by a romantically idealised great-grandfather who taught him that etiquette "guards us from all humiliation and discomfort" even if eventually noting that it is "boring, let's switch to poetry." Edward has little grasp of monetary value, itself an oddity in a consumerist society. He can't get credit because he doesn't exist. There is even an indication that he hardly needs to eat and yet much of his life revolves around the differences between food, money and social behaviour. Most telling is when Bill gives another of his fatherly aphorisms: "You can't buy the necessities of life with cookies." This is meant to show Edward the value of money and the necessity for him to charge for services rendered. But idealistically isn't love the real necessity of life? And isn't his heart actually a cookie?

Edward can be seen as the way Burton thinks of himself - as the misunderstood artist outside of conventional life, trying to fit in but doomed by his very nature to fail in the process. Edward is a compulsive creative. His works of sculpture are grandiose in scale but naive in their simplicity. Like Burton's own art Edward's has a frailty, a childish sense of wonder about it. But this beauty and simplicity can also be turned into nightmare or grotesque. One of the images that Edward creates is that of the dinosaur (there is a Loch Ness monster in the mansion's grounds and he makes a tyrannosaurus and a diplodocus for the community), popular among children and the basis for Godzilla. Edward's sculpture is not limited to topiary as he can also turn his prodigious skills to hairdressing and ice sculpture. Indeed it is in the scenes of hairdressing that we find Edward at his most creative and alluring. Edward cuts like a pro but with a speed and flair that astonishes and excites - Joyce curls her toes in ecstasy at Edward's touch ("That was the single most thrilling experience of my whole life"). When he finishes he stands back to admire his handiwork with a cocky flourish - he knows he is good.

If Edward is considered strange you should see his neighbours! Almost everyone in *Edward Scissorhands* falls into the category of exaggerated stereotype, as is befitting for a fable. Joyce is the frustrated randy housewife with appalling taste in leggings, who may be first to recognise Edward's potential, but is also the first to strike back. Often accompanied by a Tom Jones song (most notably 'Delilah') we know from the outset that her intentions are anything but honourable. Helen is the perennial gossip, orchestrating the meetings conducted at the street corner. Then there is doomsayer Esmerelda who is the first to point out that Edward is evil ("Trample down the perversion of nature"), the first to say she was right all along and spends most of her days playing an atrocious electronic organ. Unsurprisingly her eventual come-uppance reflects her fears mirrored back at her - her hedge is transformed into the head of a horned demon. Even Peg falls into the saccharine neighbour mould but her persistence and devotion to her new family member take her beyond the confines of her stereotype. It is mainly through these female characters that Edward is forced to interact, as they have the time to lavish upon him. The only real contact he has with men are Bill (who tries to explain the mysteries of women and especially his teenage daughter), Kevin (who is more impressed by the potential Edward has to deliver killer karate chops and gets him to perform a barnstorming decoupage-based Show and Tell) and Jim. Jim is everything that Edward is not. Jim is abusive, self-centred and representative of 'normal' society. He dresses in football jackets, has a pretty girlfriend, picks fights, laughs at those less fortunate than himself and is perfectly happy that someone else takes the rap for his misdemeanours. He is the epitome of modern society and his passing at the film's close is a cause for much celebration.

Edward Scissorhands again revels in a love for kooky gadgetry. The Inventor's laboratory is a paradise with huge machines chuffing away to produce, amongst other things, heart-shaped biscuits. Sugar and spice and all things nice do not only little girls make. These intricate but old-fashioned pieces of machinery seem enormously complex to produce such a basic product - they are as much machines for the sake of being machines. In this respect they have personality and purpose: little metallic robots stamp out the shapes with their cutting feet; the mixture is whisked by mechanical arms; kneaded by disembodied legs; and baked in a smiley-faced oven with bellows for ears. The Inventor's greatest achievement is Edward. Plucked from the line of robots, he is elevated to humanity. This is an inversion of the genre conventions of the mad scientist film. Normally the mad scientist figure is either a maniacal would-be ruler of the world, or a misunderstood genius messing with the forces of nature who unwittingly unleashes a beast. Whilst superficially the Inventor shares characteristics with the latter model, the Frankenstein model, he doesn't create Edward with any sense of malice or apparent medical breakthrough. He is less of a mad scientist than a Victorian inventor uncle, a sweet crank, and Edward is no monster. Although created from scratch, he is a facsimile of nature not a mockery of it. That the community goes up in arms against him as they did in *Frankenstein,* is less a reflection on him than on mob reaction in general - how little things have changed.

In *Edward Scissorhands* snow doesn't merely provide a visual motif or even a shorthand way of linking to the Christmas season but is the very purpose of the film - Edward the artist standing alone at the top of the mountain creating beautiful snow for the town below and sculpting an effigy of Kim dancing. This single image links the bookending, where an old Kim tells her grandchild about the Christmas feeling and the moment when, at their lowest ebb, Edward and Kim find unbridled happiness. Kim, finally realising she loves Edward, goes outside to see the snow falling and is enchanted when she realises it is of his making. For a few short seconds she dances in pure joy before their world collapses. A few moments perhaps, but worth a lifetime of mediocrity for them both.

Edward Scissorhands is a fable, a simple tale of unquestioning love, a moving film of elegance and beauty. It is modern Hollywood's finest film, a peerless, perfect example of the blend between art, emotion and commercial that will rightly remain as one of the select classics of cinema. Some have called it a modern masterpiece. It does not need to be quantified or excused by the expression 'modern' at all.

Style And Score: Stylistically *Edward Scissorhands* represents a continuation of the design ethics of *Beetlejuice* and *Pee-wee's Big Adventure* in its marrying of the twee and mundane with the gothic and disjointed. The distance between his mansion abode and the suburb below is more than physical - it is ideological and aesthetic. The suburban houses with their pastel colour schemes, their individuality within conformist constraints, show the community's defensive stance against anything that breaks with convention. In contrast, Edward's mansion may be dark and brooding but it is honest and a genuine home.

Although unwilling to commit himself Danny Elfman has said that the score for *Edward Scissorhands* is "one of my favourites, perhaps even my favourite" (Composer commentary) but this is far too modest. Recognising the faerie tale, the music reflects this in its sweeping trills and ethereal choral work like a magical breeze that whips up into a refreshing wind. From tinkling bells to rousing dense passages, this is the perfect marriage of music and imagery with Edward's various emotional states being emphasised by his themes. By the time the closing shot shows Edward bestowing the gift of snow on the town below, answering the inquisitive request that started the film, you are eternally grateful for Elfman's majestic music.

Making Of: Edward represents the alienation that many teenagers feel about fitting into society and in some respects this reflects Burton's coming to terms with his own childhood in Burbank. However, in order to realise the idealised version of his home town they filmed in Florida, the other side of the country. The weather in Florida was not conducive to film-making. The blistering heat made things very difficult for both the actors and crew, particularly Johnny Depp who had to perform in full costume and make-up under the blazing sun. The constantly changing skies meant that shot matching was a big problem too. However, if the heat was bad, the bugs were worse. At certain times of the day they were unable to film due to the proliferation of bugs that plagued the area, turning the set into a swarm of black. Shooting took the best part of four months during which time they commandeered the entire town, paying the residents of around 50 of the houses and putting them up at a nearby motel. Most of the interior sets in the film were contemporaneous with the houses and were changed very little. In order to get the desired look each house was repainted, but when filming was complete they were returned to their former state. Edward's mansion was built full-scale on one of the only inclines in the famously flat state but the interior was filmed on soundstages. Burton used the talents of Bo Welch to realise that grand angular interior; including the sweeping staircase and impressive machinery. What is uncommon about *Edward Scissorhands* is that much of what you see onscreen was completed in-camera and not the result of extensive post-production work or miniatures. For example, the Inventor's cookie machine was, to all intents and purposes, fully functional with the exception that it couldn't actually make cookies. One of the first things that was created in pre-production was Edward's hands, in order for Johnny Depp to have adequate time to learn how to use them. Indeed some of the scars on his face are not make-up! Even though Burton gave Depp his big break, things were not easy for the young actor. Apart from the hands themselves there was the costume to contend with as well as the climate. In the barbecue scene where a kebab-handed Edward is fed ambrosia salad, Johnny had to endure the ordeal for a full twenty takes, the result of which was a very sick actor.

Making Of You Don't Want To Know: Naturally snow doesn't come every day to Florida so it needed to be manufactured using real ice shavings, bits of plastic and other glittery things to get the required sparkle on film. For the tear-jerkingly beautiful sequence of Kim dancing in the snow, they filmed partly on location and, in order to get the cold feeling right, partly in a meat freezer. How romantic...

The Creation: The concept for *Edwards Scissorhands* originally came from a drawing that Burton had created in his teens. At that time Edward did not have scissors for hands, merely sharp instruments - the character was unable to hold anything that he loved for fear of damaging it. Burton had wanted to do something with the drawing for some time but was unable to find either the backing or the inspiration to realise it. Eventually he turned to scriptwriter Caroline Thompson who immediately empathised with the character and set about making a story. As Thompson says "It's a fable. A fable is a story that people don't necessarily believe but they understand. You understand what it's about because what it's about is a feeling like you don't belong and feeling like you want to belong and feeling like you're trying to belong and feeling like you should belong and you can't belong." Key to the film's strength is her erudite and free-flowing script, and it's easy to see why Burton would find her skills so much in tune with his, for her own tales have centred on the macabre and the outsider. Her novel, *First Born*, concerned the adventures of an aborted foetus. Later she would provide the script for *The Nightmare Before Christmas*. Continuing the combination of 'strange but loving', she co-wrote (with Larry *Beetlejuice* Wilson) the screenplay for Barry Sonnenfeld's finest film *The Addams Family* (1991) where Charles Addams' family of ghoulish misfits are treated as far more preferable to anyone in normal money-grabbing society. This ability to make something generally considered socially unacceptable or disgusting into something that audiences can care about, and even empathise with, is one of her many talents.

Aftermath: Vincent Price's career had covered over half a century, providing audiences with chills, thrills and humour. His distinctive voice and impeccable manners were an inspiration to many. Burton had always wanted to work with his hero, indeed if Vincent Price had not been so generous with the director's first foray into film-making (*Vincent*) his career may well have taken a totally different path. Burton's collaboration with his idol continued after filming *Edward Scissorhands,* as he wanted to show the world Price's versatility and compassion. *Conversations With Vincent* (as it has been preliminarily named) is a series of interviews conducted by Burton about Price's career. Hopefully this long gestating project will eventually see the light of day.

Trivia: At the barbecue there is a cameo by Stuart Lancaster, one of the stars of Russ Meyer's *Faster Pussycat! Kill! Kill!* (1966). When Johnny Depp was given the role he was not an established star or household name. He was at that time known primarily for TV roles and a part in Wes Craven's *A Nightmare On Elm Street* (1984) where he fell foul of the man with razors for fingers.

The Verdict: 5/5

Bats, Cats And An Army That Quacks

"I don't know about you Miss Kitty but I feel so much... yummier."

Warner Brothers were trying to keep the ball rolling on their huge money-spinner, and had been keen to get Burton on board to do a sequel to *Batman* almost as soon as it was released. However Burton stood his ground, agreeing to return to the series if he was allowed to go off and make a personal project. *Edward Scissorhands* completed, the job of returning to the DC hero became a reality. The intervening couple of years had enhanced Burton's ability to handle huge budgets and crew. He also retained final cut providing he deliver a film with no more than a PG-13 rating. Because of this, *Batman Returns* is the best Batman film to date and far more satisfying than the original. It doesn't balk on the action set pieces, explosions and fight scenes demanded by popcorn munchers, but adds to the formula that makes the viewing experience so rewarding.

Batman Returns (1992)

Crew: Dir: Tim Burton, Prd: Denise Di Novi, Tim Burton, Co-Prd: Larry Franco, Exec Prd: Jon Peters, Peter Guber, Benjamin Melniker, Michael Uslan, Story: Daniel Waters, Sam Hamm, Scr: Daniel Waters, DP: Stefan Czapsky, Music: Danny Elfman, 121 mins

Cast: Michael Keaton (Batman/Bruce Wayne), Danny de Vito (The Penguin/Oswald Cobblepot), Michelle Pfeiffer (Catwoman/Selina Kyle), Christopher Walken (Max Shreck), Pat Hingle (Commissioner Gordon), Michael Gough (Alfred), Michael Murphy (Mayor), Cristi Conaway (Ice Princess), Andrew Bryniarski (Chip Shreck)

Plot: Christmas time, mistletoe and crime. Those long-suffering citizens of Gotham city are facing a Christmas without pomp and ceremony. Sure there's a big tree but who's going to wait to see its lights turned on when the city is under the vice-like grip of urban terrorism? Gotham needs a stronger leader than the insipid mayor to instil confidence in the flagging power structure and rid the streets of filth. Who could possibly fit the demanding post? There is one candidate that springs to mind - who would be ideal to have the city in the palm of his flipper - the Penguin. Long considered to be an urban myth, the Penguin was abandoned by his rich parents because of his unique deformities and erratic behaviour. Left to drift in the sewers, he survived in the company of his peers at the zoo. His return to the world above ground is triumphal, rescuing the current mayor's child from the hands of an unscrupulous kidnapper (how does he know the kidnapper is unscrupulous? Because he got him to do the job in the first place) and straight onto the front pages. What he needs though is someone with a touch more business acumen than his loyal Red Triangle Circus Gang and army of dedicated penguins. This is where Max Shreck comes in. Max is a shrewd entrepreneur with big plans for the city, plans that will be mightily beneficial to his financial well-being and that of his vacant son Chip. By backing the Penguin's ascension he can get the permission he needs to build a power plant with a difference. Most power plants, you see, generate power but Shreck's ingenious plan would see its role as a giant capacitor, soaking up resources to be put to his doubtless nefarious schemes. However, his dastardly plan is unwittingly uncovered by his lonely, bumbling and insecure secretary (sorry, office assistant) Selina Kyle. Stupidly revealing to Shreck that she has figured out his cunning plan, she finds her way from the top of Shreck's very tall building to the ground floor in record time, and she didn't take the lift. Left for dead, she is revived by a group of passing alley cats and stumbles back to her twee apartment. There she feverishly works on a new identity - sleek, deadly, amoral - Catwoman.

The Penguin, meanwhile, has been searching for his roots - discovering that he is actually Oswald Cobblepot, son and heir of a rich deceased couple that were pillar stones of Gotham's upper echelons. With the backing of Shreck he is transformed from his raw fish eating, thermal-underweared self into a slick, top hat and suit gentleman, able to hold himself in front of the plethora of television cameras and news photographers.

But what, you may ask, of the caped crusader? Well, our cave-dwelling millionaire crime fighter is carrying on with business as usual; fighting crime in all its infernal incarnations when the sky is illuminated by the bat signal. Things have been a bit hectic recently, what with the wave of criminal activity executed by the Red Triangle Circus Gang and the emergence of wild card Catwoman (who is now in cahoots with the Penguin due to her love/hate relationship with Batman). To facilitate an early election the terrible trio of Penguin, Catwoman and Shreck devise a way of not only discrediting the current office but also their law-enforcing bat-winged linchpin. Implicating him in the kidnap and murder of bubbly but vacuum-brained model Ice Princess, he is disgraced live on television when the Batmobile runs amok, driving indiscriminately into civilians with little attention to the Highway Code. But Batman is a wily devil and turns the tables on the Penguin, ruining his chances at office and reinstating himself as the de facto protector of the common man. You would think that all would be well but Hell hath no fury like a Penguin riled and he runs to ground to launch an all-out apocalyptic attack on the city from which no one, not even Shreck, Catwoman, Commissioner Gordon or Batman, will be exempt. If that were not enough, Bruce Wayne is having to come to terms with the fact that the woman he loves (Selina) and the woman he loves to hate to love (Catwoman) are one and the same...

"*Batman Returns* is not really a sequel to *Batman*. It doesn't pick up where the first film left off... The point was to make it all feel fresh and new."

Tim Burton, from the Introduction to *Batman Returns: The Official Movie Book*.

Comment: Obviously comparisons with the first film are inevitable and, once again, it seems as though the titular character plays not second but at least third fiddle to the villains. But both stylistically and ideologically this is far removed from the original. Fundamental to the film is the emotional and physical relationship between Batman and Catwoman, a tempestuous and fetishistic romance of the kind you rarely see in a Hollywood film. Batman remains an enigma (the strong silent shape, dealing vengeance to wrongdoers) so his presence is always felt but not explicitly seen. He is Gotham's omnipotent protector and as such his vigilante behaviour operates in the shadows. His nemeses are far more flamboyant but ultimately they are similar to him. The exception is Shreck (the only real bad guy), who doesn't don some kind of disguise or have a split personality. To this end he is the most normal, the most respectable and the most dangerous of criminals. Maybe the Penguin's wrath unleashed would be more damaging but it is the result of instinct, of uncontrollable natural urge. Shreck is calculating and people suffer as a result of his irrepressible corporate greed.

There is a sense that Selina's fate and rebirth as Catwoman is preordained. Indeed there is a streak of fatalism that runs throughout the film. The characters are so tied up in their own psyches that any deviation ends in tragedy or reversion. Even before she has been unceremoniously shoved out of Shreck's building, Selina is referred to in cat terms ("I'm afraid we haven't properly housebroken Miss Kyle", "What did curiosity do to the cat?"). After her reinvention she takes on the characteristics of a cat; amoral and unpredictable. She wrecks her own furniture, trashes her pad and paints her doll's house black. The tacky neon sign in her otherwise pastel bedroom is smashed to read not "HELLO THERE" but "HELL HERE." She creates her costume from PVC and fashions razor-sharp nails to gouge and slash. In contrast to Batman's functional logically-designed suit, manufactured to exacting tailored standards, Catwoman's is elemental, intuitive and the result of delirious labour. She causes childlike vandalism in a store, decapitating dummies with a well-aimed whip or contemptuously dealing with inept security guards before blowing the place sky high by imaginative use of a microwave - meow. When she encounters Batman the screen really lights up. Despite (or because of) the fact they are both clad almost entirely from head to toe, the scenes crackle with intense erotic charge. Both are extreme fetishists who dress up to express their sexual drive in a way they find incapable of doing in their 'normal' everyday guises. Their multitude of fights are thinly disguised sexual play. They relate romantically through mutual pain. Batman's rubber may not be real under Catwoman's touch but she likes it. Similarly her apparel is that of a Gothic dominatrix who teases her prey. Batman has designed half of his house to be a fetishist's paradise - he has a dungeon to skulk in and gets there by means of an iron maiden entrance. Alfred just uses the stairs. After his first big fight with Catwoman, Batman requests that Alfred bring him some anti-septic so that he may dress his considerable wounds. "Are you in pain sir?" he asks. "No," comes the reply. When Bruce Wayne and Selina finally realise their opposite's alter ego the tension is part relief and part concern as to the future of their sadomasochistic relationship. Indeed Selina declares: "Does this mean we have to start fighting?" half in hope, half in despair. That they discover each other's identities at a masked ball, whilst not wearing their masks, is an irony that is not lost on them. Masks again play a great deal of importance, both as part of their fetish games and to free the id of the wearer. Both Batman and Catwoman function better with their masks on. Thus they are more passionate lovers grappling on rooftops - Catwoman licking the face of Batman - than they can ever be getting cosy by the fire at Wayne mansion or waltzing at a big cheese social event.

The Penguin is the real tragedy figure of the piece because he is misguided and elemental, another force of nature. Catwoman and Batman can survive dual (or should that be duel?) personality, but not so the Penguin. Rejected at birth, he is cast from a bridge and ends up in the sewers. These scenes are shot in almost black and white to emphasise the tortured and gothic start to his unfortunate origins. Despite the fact that Batman is psychologically com-pelled to become a man-beast there is no physiological reason for him to do so (nor Catwoman for that matter) but the Penguin is forced to live with his hor-rific appearance. As he accurately points out, "I'm a genuine freak and you're just someone wearing a mask." Not that, like rich kid Batman, he is without his toys. The Penguin's impressive array of functional yet stylish umbrellas get him out of many sticky situations - either as handy guns, a helicopter, gas dispensers or just a means of invoking a really nasty headache. His gadgets are more toylike than Batman's, perhaps reflecting the childhood he never had. His moving declaration that, "I am a man. I have a name. Oswald Cob-blepot," is tainted by his realisation that his parents rejected him - "I was their number one son and they treated me like number two." He concludes the film, and his life, knowing who he really is: "I am not a human being, I am an ani-mal."

Style And Score: Thankfully we are back almost entirely in Danny Elfman land and what a relief it is. Bar a few moments in the ballroom scene and a surprisingly average Siouxsie And The Banshee's number over the end cred-its, the bombastic superiority of Elfman's score is all the music you need, energetically conducted by Oingo Boingo guitarist Steve Bartek. The intervening years also saw a vast improvement in sound technology with the overall effect that *Batman Returns* is far more immersive and exhilarating than its predecessor.

Burton turned to Bo Welch to design the extravagant sets and his Disney buddy Heinrichs to contribute to the art direction. The results are breathtaking in their scale as well as design. The Gotham Plaza set alone was a massive 65 foot in height, complete with huge futurist (half-Soviet half-Nazi looking) statues sculpted by Leo Rijn and 35-foot-high Christmas trees dressed with lights. The colour palette once again is dark and gloomy comprising muted colours contrasting with the Penguin's bright toys. Most of the film was produced on soundstages which adds an aura of dreamlike unreality that some people find stagy, others magical. It also allows the lighting cameraman complete control over the environment, where colour and fluidity of camera movement are paramount, unshackled by the real world. As much as Burton's films are based outside of reality, so many of them are actually filmed outside of reality! Cinematographer Stefan Czapsky proved once again that he is the man to hire if you want snow to look dreamy.

Making Of: Having ditched the prospect of reusing the sets from the first film, Burton also decided not to film the sequel in the UK. He used the Warner soundstages at Burbank to construct the vast sets. The Penguin's lair had to be built on the 'modest' 50-foot soundstage and kept filled with 25,000 gallons of water. No animals were harmed and their comfort came before the cast and crew, who had to film in temperatures just above freezing point.

Sets alone do not make a film. A good deal of effort went into realising the astonishing array of ideas. For example, real penguins were used for the hordes of penguins but, as with most animals, they found it difficult to hit their marks on cue, so many of the shots are a combination of people in costumes, CGI and animatronics. The animatronics were handled by the Stan Winston Workshop. CGI was employed for the crowd scenes of penguins, the swarms of bats and the Batmobile's shield which had been hand animated in the first film. The leap in affordable CGI in a scant couple of years was such that it could be employed more extensively. Other aspects however, such as the Bat-ski, were created by more traditional modelling techniques. Also, much of the film relies on the ancient and distinguished art of the matte painting to give depth and perspective.

Batground: Having dealt with Batman's most famous foe in the original, *Batman Returns* pits the caped crusader against two other well-known adversaries, Catwoman and The Penguin. In the Adam West TV series, the Penguin was memorably played by Burgess Meredith. Catwoman was played by three actresses: Julie Newmar, Lee Meriwether (who played in the feature version *Batman* (1966)) and Eartha Kitt. Both characters had originated in Bob

Kane's comics: Catwoman made her first appearance in 1940 and the Penguin the following year. Catwoman was originally based on a cross between Kane's girlfriend at the time (whose seamstress skills also fed into the character) and popular actresses Hedy Lamarr and Jean Harlow, while the Penguin came from an inspirational packet of Kool cigarettes. Probably a good thing Kane didn't smoke Camels instead...

Trivia: *Batman Returns* was once again rated 12 in the UK, but this time cuts were made in order to comply with the BBFC's occasionally bizarre policies of the time. First to go were the clown's nunchuka, which were weapons routinely removed from virtually every film from the mid-1970s to the late 1990s. The other cut was Catwoman's use of aerosol cans in a microwave as an explosive device, because of concerns that the action could encourage imitation. Irritating though the fleeting nunchuka cut is, the end result is hardly noticeable but in the case of the aerosol, the sequence makes little causal sense and Catwoman's well-timed "Meow" seems the work of good fortune rather than a planned outburst. In the States these scenes hardly warranted a mention. They were more concerned about the film's moral angle and the fact that the Penguin spews black bile from his mouth - warranting a PG-13 only after substantial cuts.

Christopher Walken's Max Shreck character is named after the creepy looking actor (Max Schreck) who played the titular role in *Nosferatu*, a seminal example of German expressionist horror cinema. Burton was not keen to continue making *Batman* films after this but did spend some time working on a possible spin-off featuring Catwoman, a part which he considered had more potential for moral ambiguity. Sadly the project fell through. Seen briefly in the pre-credit sequence the aristocratic Tucker Cobblepot is played by none other than Paul Reubens, aka Pee-wee Herman. His 'wife' is Diane Salinger, who played Simone in *Pee-wee's Big Adventure*.

The Verdict: 5/5

Although *Batman Returns* smashed box-office records for first weekend takings, its popularity quickly declined because audiences were simply not expecting such a dark vision. This was not a good time for Burton - his marriage was not going well. He served as producer on such projects as *The Nightmare Before Christmas* and *Cabin Boy*. During the making of *The Nightmare Before Christmas* he met model Lisa Marie and the pair connected almost immediately. She would feature in every subsequent Burton film.

Angora, Bela, Cinema: The ABC Of Ed Wood

> "Can your hearts stand the shocking facts of the true story of
> Edward D Wood Jr.?"

Writers Scott Alexander and Larry Karaszewski had wanted to make a film about Edward D Wood Jr. for some time. They had even planned a documentary while they were at Film School, originally entitled *The Man With The Angora Sweater*. The pair earned their reputation by penning the *Problem Child* films but were disgruntled by the studios' handling of their material so sought to revive their Ed Wood project, turning to buddy Michael Lehmann, director of the excellent Di Novi-produced black comedy *Heathers*. Lehmann was interested in directing, passed the treatment to Di Novi who showed it to Burton for his opinion. Burton enthused so much about the project that a deal was struck - Lehmann would step down (receiving credit as executive producer) if Burton made the film as his next project without further development delays. The only snags were that the script itself hadn't actually been written and Burton was in pre-production on *Mary Reilly* for Columbia. Eventually he managed to get released from the project in favour of the quickly-written *Ed Wood*. Initially Columbia agreed to put up the money for the new film, but the studio bigwigs were not entirely sure about the subject matter and eventually pulled out once they heard that Burton insisted that it be shot in black and white. Instead Touchstone fronted the budget as they had on their other Burton/Di Novi ventures, *The Nightmare Before Christmas* and *Cabin Boy*.

Ed Wood (1994)

Crew: Dir: Tim Burton, Prd: Tim Burton, Denise Di Novi, Exec Prd: Michael Lehmann, Scr: Scott Alexander, Larry Karaszewski, DP: Stefan Czapsky, Music: Howard Shore, 121 mins

Cast: Johnny Depp (Ed Wood), Martin Landau (Bela Lugosi), Sarah Jessica Parker (Dolores Fuller), Bill Murray (Bunny Breckinridge), Lisa Marie (Vampira), Patricia Arquette (Kathy), Jeffrey Jones (Criswell), Vincent D'Onofrio (Orson Welles)

Plot: Underneath the comforting, enveloping folds of the Hollywood sign a play is premiered – *The Casual Company*, a war fable with fantasy sequences and lyrical dialogue. Its writer/director is Ed Wood, proud of his play and the good work shown by his dedicated actors. Not everyone sees it that way though - the reviews are awful, despite the fact the critics had failed to turn up. Most people would be disheartened by rejection but not Ed. He has big plans for working in the movies. Spotting an article on the proposed filming of *I Changed My Sex,* Wood plucks up the courage to face producer George Weiss and pitch his desire to write and direct the picture. Weiss is an exploitation producer who films, in his own words, "crap" to sell to undiscerning drive-ins and flea pits. Ed reveals the fact that he is qualified to take on the task because he is a transvestite and can understand the motivation for the central character, but Weiss turns him down. As luck would have it through, Ed bumps into veteran horror actor Bela Lugosi at a local funeral parlour. Bela hasn't had a job in years and has been shirked by the industry because of his morphine habit, but Ed sees potential in him whilst realising that he could be the pull needed to get the job. It works and Ed gets together an enthusiastic team to film the newly retitled (unknown to Weiss) *Glen Or Glenda,* casting himself in the lead role as a man obsessed with women's clothing. If only he'd told his girlfriend Dolores the truth behind his personal interest - she's not happy to discover why her angora sweaters keep disappearing.

Glen Or Glenda is a roaring success. To Wood. Everyone else thinks it stinks but, flushed with enthusiasm, he starts on his next project: *Bride Of The Atom.* Although he initially manages to generate some interest in Hollywood, the moment producers see *Glen Or Glenda* the doors shut. Instead he tries organising fund-raising parties with his buddies, including wrestling sensation Tor Johnson and hopefully soon-to-be woman Bunny. All seems doomed until he finds Loretta King, who agrees to fund the picture in return for a lead status, hence ousting Dolores from a part written specifically for her. But Loretta turns out not to have any money after all and Ed finishes *Bride Of The Atom* thanks to a grant given by the owner of the McCoy Meat Packing facility on the condition that it ends with an explosion and features McCoy's son Tony. But this joy is short lived – Dolores leaves Ed and Lugosi ends up in rehabilitation, prompting interest from the press for the first time in nearly a decade. Following his release, Ed steps in to give Bela hope and begins shooting a new film with the ageing star, but Bela finally passes away and is laid to rest.

The death of your lead is normally a setback but for Ed the opportunity to immortalise the memory of his friend is too strong. With the help of Kathy, his new beau who he met while Bela was in the clinic, Bunny, Tor, Criswell the psychic, the newly out-of-a-job Vampira and the rest of the gang, they set about creating what will surely be Ed's masterpiece, his magnum opus: *Grave Robbers From Outer Space.* The only thing they need to do before photography can begin is to find an identical body double for Bela and get baptised...

"There's something beautiful about somebody who does what they love to do, no matter how misguided, and remains upbeat and optimistic against all odds."

Tim Burton, *Cinefantastique* April 1994

Comment: *Ed Wood* takes the biopic formula and subverts it by concentrating on someone who was spectacularly unsuccessful. It is so easy to see how this material could have become a sneering mocking comedy, laughing at someone else's ineptitude, but fortunately it doesn't. Yes, the film ignores some of the more unpleasant aspects of his tale but internally it remains coherent - Ed was a dreamer and the film reflects this. If Wood had believed his films and writing were of no value he would not have continued, and so he is portrayed as a misguided visionary. All biopics take liberties with the source material and this is no exception. Characters have necessarily been trimmed, amalgamated and altered in the name of narrative purity but there is a sense in which the spirit seems right. Although the film wisely sticks to one relatively brief period in his life from the inception of his first major film to his masterpiece, the writers take their biggest liberty when Ed meets his idol, Orson Welles. Factually inaccurate, the scene represents the ethos of the film: despite many setbacks Ed is encouraged to stick to his guns and realise his unique vision. The irony of one of America's most critically-lauded directors (*Citizen Kane* still, for want of bothering to be controversial, appears at the top of most critics' lists) empathising with one of its most despised is not lost. Hollywood failed to understand Welles as much as they failed to understand Wood, for entirely different reasons. Welles points out that "Visions are worth fighting for. Why spend your life living someone else's dreams?" and Eddie, suitably invigorated, goes to the première of *Plan 9 From Outer Space*. That the film should end on a triumphal note continues in the tradition of the biopic. Thus *Ed Wood* ends with Ed's most gloriously renowned achievement.

Ed Wood is an actor's piece with roles offering a wonderful opportunity for expression. Johnny Depp proves once again that in the right part he is peerless – as Ed his conviction and unstoppable enthusiasm burst upon every frame. He is so impassioned that he mouths every line of his dialogue, relishing every poetic nuance, emphasising meaning with expressive eyebrows and nods. Then there is the Oscar-winning performance from Martin Landau under make-up from Rick Baker's team that is so good you don't even realise it is make-up – alternating between despair, desperately brandishing a gun, enthusiastically relishing the chance to act again or exploding with rage any time someone mentions Boris Karloff ("Karloff? Sidekick? Fuck you!"). Similarly, the supporting roles are perfectly fleshed out – Dolores' lack of understanding of Ed's needs coupled with his inability to deal with hers. Her final scene in his films is a mere walk-on - the shrivelling glance she gives the camera looks just like the real thing. There's Vampira contemptuously accepting her part as though it's beneath her, played by wince-inducing corseted Lisa Marie. Jeffrey Jones is crankily aristocratic as posh-voiced TV psychic Criswell. Patricia Arquette is touching as Kathy, while Vincent D'Onofrio's Orson Welles is uncanny in likeness and mannerism. But best of all is a show-stopping turn from Bill Murray as Bunny Breckinridge who manages to be decadently camp without 'over-mincing' the part, always surreptitiously eyeing up any passing hunk, planning his operation in Mexico and splashing around in dismay at his undignified baptism.

It's the incidentals and details that make *Ed Wood* so eminently watchable and quotable. There's the colour-blind cameraman who, when asked which dress will look best declares, "the dark grey one." The walk through a Hollywood set with a huge plant (shades of *Pee-wee's Big Adventure*) culminating in Ed's discovery of the joys of stock footage. Then there's the casting of Tom the chiropractor as Bela's stand-in because they have similar looking ears... but nothing else alike. Tor and his family. The premiere disaster of *Bride Of The Atom*. Stealing the octopus. "Pull de strings!" Learning the hypnotic hand trick. "Get me transvestites, I need transvestites!" The poor TV comedy sketch show that humiliates Bela. Criswell predicts. The hilarious baptism. "I haf no home." Ignoring the wobbly sets. Filming the flying saucers on fire. "Where's my pink sweater?" The party in McCoy's meat plant. There's so much crammed into the running time, and all of it based 'only on the sworn testaments...'

Key to the film's humanising angle is the relationship between director Wood and his childhood idol, horror star Bela Lugosi. Burton had, of course, worked with his childhood idol, horror star Vincent Price, and his chosen genre of science fiction/fantasy/horror was similar to the fields Wood liked to work in.

> "Both Ed and Tim had worshipped the respective horror stars when they were young boys. Then they had met the actors and finally gotten to work with them at the end of their lives. This gave our movie an emotional foundation which we felt Tim would empathise."
>
> Scott Alexander and Larry Karaszewski,
> *Ed Wood*, Faber and Faber

Critically *Ed Wood* is Burton's most well-received film and with good reason. It won Oscars for Martin Landau (who received many more accolades, including a Golden Globe) and Rick Baker's make-up team who did such a marvellous job bringing Lugosi back to life. The London Film Critics Circle gave a Best Actor award to Johnny Depp and elsewhere Stefan Czapsky's cinematography and Howard Shore's elegant score were similarly rewarded. Yet despite this, the film did relatively poor business at the US box office, barely scraping together $5 million including a post-Oscar re-release and enthusiastic reviews. In contrast *Batman Returns* earned nearly ten times this amount in its first three days of release! Perhaps the distribution was to blame or perhaps it was because the public could not be convinced to go and see a black and white film about an artistic failure who befriends an old drug addict. If so, it is entirely their loss.

Style And Score: To date this is Burton's only feature film not to have a Danny Elfman score, a situation he commented on: "We're taking a little vacation from each other" (*Burton On Burton*). So *Ed Wood* was left in the capable hands of Howard Shore. Shore's prolific output has always been consistently good, but he is possibly best known for his collaborations with David Cronenberg. In *Ed Wood* the score is grand, as befits Ed's ideas (indeed many of the score's themes are derived from Ed's films). Like the rest of the film it never seeks to belittle him. This adds immeasurably to the film's earnestness although it is never afraid to trail an accentuating riff whenever something notably comedic happens. Most moving is the adoption of variations from Tchaikovsky's *Swan Lake* during the scenes where Ed finds Bela collapsed in a state of drug-addled illness. In many ways, whilst Danny Elfman's music is ideally suited to Burton's other work, its adoption here could easily have overwhelmed the pathos of the picture and reduced the overall impact.

One of the key decisions in making *Ed Wood* was to film in black and white. Despite being the norm for debut and low-budget Indie films, it is generally frowned upon as box-office disaster. Black and white has a nostalgic feel and a contradictory visual reaction between realism (we are used to seeing old documentaries in black and white) and dreamlike (in fiction it is detached from the Hollywood norm and therefore brings attention to itself). *Ed Wood*'s use of chiaroscuro lighting to increase dramatic tension, especially in the low-angle shots that recall 1950s film noir, emphasises the psychological states of the characters. When Ed returns in the middle of the night to the pleading Bela following a collapse, the extremity of the angles increases on each visit until finally, when Bela has died, the camera tilts slowly from side to side like a drunk. The emotional horror of the situation is expressed in camera movement and shadow. It would be difficult to convey the same kind of psychology in colour. Also, filming in black and white recreates the stock of Ed's films up to this point in his career.

The titles are perhaps most indicative of Wood as a film-maker, employing all the elements of his films in one (apparently) single shot following the *Plan 9* style introduction from Criswell in his coffin. Swooping down over graveyards, past underwater octopi and encompassing flying saucers and lightning strikes, the spooky pastiche music and sense of wholesome cheesiness prevail. It ends up on the famous Hollywood sign before craning down to Ed's first theatre production.

Can't See The Wood: Edward D Wood Jr. has gone down in the annals of film history as the worst director of all time, an honour brought to wider attention in *The Golden Turkey Awards* written by the Medved brothers. The Medveds' combination of condescension and ridicule now seems decidedly mean spirited but ultimately their scornful attitude (Wood was awarded Worst Director and *Plan 9 From Outer Space* worst film) has backfired in that the films of Ed Wood are now readily available on video and have been seen by more people now than during his lifetime. Interest in Wood started in the 1980s, and continues to the present day, as eager fans tried to unearth missing films, fragments of projects and the prodigious amount of fiction he wrote. On top of the films already known to fans, *Night Of The Ghouls* (1959) was unearthed, paid for (it had remained with the developers when funds were not available to have the print finished) and released. Some of his novels (including *Killer In Drag* and *Death Of A Transvestite*) were also reprinted. Author Rudolph Grey interviewed the surviving members of Wood's entourage to produce a collage of recollections about the man, his life and his films. The book *Visions Of Ecstasy: The Life And Art Of Edward D Wood Jr.* provided the background material for Scott Alexander and Larry Karaszewski to develop their script. There was also an excellent television documentary, *Look Back In Angora*, which incorporated stock footage along with interviews. Wood had finally made it big time.

Ed Wood's life was as fascinating as his films. Born in Poughkeepsie on October 10, 1924, he served in the US Marines during World War II and fought hard in the invasion of Tarawa. During one of America's most bloody battles he was wearing women's underwear underneath his combats. His valour on the battlefield (only 10% of those going in came out) resulted in a decoration and the loss of his front teeth, smashed out with a rifle butt. Wood was a heterosexual transvestite with a particular predilection for angora, but more importantly he was a man who strove to realise his dream of becoming a Hollywood director. A prolific writer, Wood turned his hand to short stories, novels, screenplays and theatre work. He moved from directing unsuccessful plays to directing unsuccessful films when given the chance to make a cheap exploitation flick about the Christine Jorgensen sex change case. Wood took the opportunity to put his indelible stamp on the project (he even took the title role under a pseudonym, one of the very few times he did use a false name, even when working in the porno industry) turning the film into a pot-pourri of disingenuous ideas, surreal dream sequences and stock footage. It also marked the start of his relationship with Bela Lugosi. He continued making pictures and writing them, from crime thrillers like *Jailbait* to his magnum opus *Grave*

Robbers From Outer Space (aka *Plan 9 From Outer Space*). Following this, his career took a downslide including work on a bizarre horror strip-flick *Orgy Of The Dead*. By the 1970s he had turned to making porno movies and 'educational' sex films sold as part-works. He wrote all the time and drank heavily. On December 10, 1978, he passed away. He never knew of the glorious renaissance of his work.

When initially watching the films of Ed Wood the criticisms about his film-making (day and night intercuts, ropey sets, dubious acting etc.) are easy to scoff at, but a number of things strike you once you've become immersed in his world. The stories, no matter how preposterous or badly filmed, are always engaging. The dialogue (often quoted as appalling) occasionally touches brilliance, but ultimately works better written down. Despite any shortcomings they are infinitely more interesting and watchable than the slew of relentlessly average low-budget films made in the same period. Ed Wood's films engage even at their worst and are undeniably stamped with the mark of their author. He was an American auteur who at least realised part of his dreams.

The Verdict: 5/5

Do Not Run, We Are Your Friends

"Aakk. Aaaakk ak-ak-akk, aakk akk-aak"

Mars Attacks! (1996)

Crew: Dir: Tim Burton, Prd: Tim Burton, Larry Franco, Scr: Jonathan Gems, DP: Peter Suschitzky, Music: Danny Elfman (with the inestimable aid of Slim Whitman and Tom Jones), 101 mins

Cast: Jack Nicholson (President Dale/Art Land), Glenn Close (Marsha Dale), Annette Bening (Barbara Land), Pierce Brosnan (Professor Donald Kessler), Danny de Vito (Rude Gambler), Martin Short (Jerry Ross), Sarah Jessica Parker (Nathalie Lake), Natalie Portman (Taffy Dale), Jim Brown (Byron Williams), Lukas Haas (Richie), Michael J Fox (Jason Stone), Lisa Marie (Martian Girl), Rod Steiger (General Decker), Tom Jones (Himself), Sylvia Sidney (Grandma Norris), Paul Winfield (General Casey), Pam Grier (Louise Williams), Poppy (Poppy)

Plot: It is a moving and deeply significant day in the history of humankind. A day that will live in the hearts and minds of our children and our children's children. This day we found out we are not alone - there is life on Mars. Thousands of super-technological spaceships hover around our fair planet like bees to their hive. Top scientist Professor Donald Kessler reflects the optimistic views of many. This is a race so advanced, so intelligent, so enlightened that they must be peaceful, wanting to extend the hand, paw or tentacle of extraterrestrial friendship. Perhaps they can learn from our culture as much as we can surely learn from theirs. The instruments to perform rudimentary translation are ready and the location for the momentous first meeting between man and Martian is set – Pahrump in the Nevada desert. There are of course dissenting voices in the shape of brusque General Decker and Donut World worker Richie's trailer trash parents, but deep down a special relationship is destined to be forged. The President of the United States sends the sympathetic General Casey to welcome the Martian emissary and hordes of people descend upon the desert to get a glimpse of the alien entourage. There are reporters, TV crews and a full military welcome. The majestic metallic ship lands and unfurls a "silver ramp like a giant tongue," down which the resplendent ambassador descends, attended by his guards. "We come in peace," he declares to the jubilant throng. A dove is sent heavenward and flies into the beam of a Martian ray gun that decimates its feathery body and unceremoniously dumps its smouldering corpse in front of a horrified crowd. Not that they have too long to be horrified, as the little green fellows unleash molten Martian mayhem, massacring the powerless gathering, reducing human bodies to ashen, smoking green skeletons, twisted in the ravages of death.

Sorry. Sorry. Big mistake. Customs, interspatial special differences, you know the thing. Cultural misunderstanding, if you will. The aliens arrange to address Congress as partial atonement. This is to be a strictly 'no bird' affair mind - you can't be sure what will affect alien sensibilities. But the world watches live as the venerable group are turned into human kebabs. Call it a Congress searing. The President manfully tries to put a brave face on it: "two out of three branches of the government are working and that ain't bad."

It seems as though nothing can stop the nefarious designs these intergalactic terrorists have for our world. Nothing is taboo, nothing too devious. Their only aim is domination. The good Professor, as well as flirty reporter Nathalie and Poppy the dog, are subjected to deranged medical experiments at the lime green hands of Martian doctors. Nothing is safe. They try to infiltrate the White House. They mercilessly crush boy scouts, vandalise shopfronts, decimate sites of special heritage. The Eiffel Tower? Gone. Big Ben? Will chime no more. Taj Mahal? You get the picture. Perhaps there is one final drastic course of action left to be taken by the great leaders of this world. It is harsh. It is savage. It is a terrible decision to make: all-out nuclear confrontation. The President finally decides to obliterate the invading horde using tactical nuclear devices. Surely a sorry end to what must once have been a noble race. Nope, the bombs are absolutely useless. The invasion continues with renewed vigour. Goodbye Mr President.

So, no hope for the world. The end is nigh. Mankind has ceased to be. Hey, hang on, just because the top brass haven't sorted out a solution it doesn't mean that no one else can. There are a lot of plucky people out there who love the world too. There's Richie and his senile grandma, estranged couple Byron and Louise Williams (their kids have managed to whoop Martian butt and save the White House while the internal security floundered like imbeciles) and top singing sensation Tom Jones. With heroes like these surely the future of the world is in safe hands?

Comment: Mars Attacks! may differ on the surface from the rest of Burton's canon but it retains elements that are clearly his. The basic story concerns the outsiders as the most important figures. The President is insignificant compared with the disenfranchised ordinary folk - the hardworking mother, her ex-boxer husband with his strict moral code, a wheelchair-bound OAP (who talks lovingly to her stuffed cat called Muffy), the President's daughter who actually cares for her country's history and a gangly donut store worker who dreams of a non-militaristic US free of the dismissive parents who prefer his 'normal' brother. Also, the appreciation of horror films that runs throughout *Edward Scissorhands* (quality) and *Ed Wood* (bargain basement) sees its fullest expression here, as does his lifelong love of *Godzilla* films. Indeed, *Mars Attacks!* features a clip of the big G in one of his more recent excursions (*Godzilla Vs. Biollante*) to emphasise the connection. Like the Japanese films, *Mars Attacks!* features the audience-pleasing thrills of seeing major cities wiped out for no reason other than to entertain. Thus we see Las Vegas get trashed, followed by a world tour. *Mars Attacks!* was often compared with *Independence Day* (1996) which likewise follows the President and a large entourage of bit players 'from all walks of life' coping with a violent alien invasion. What that film also contains is scene after scene of jingoistic rhetoric, tedious children, dialogue that is only 'witty' when delivered for macho posturing purposes and contains the most shameful patriotic rallying speech since *Henry V*. At least *Mars Attacks!* has the decency to acknowledge its forbears whilst injecting copious and much welcomed humour, rather than acting as bland propaganda masquerading as art/entertainment.

Another key element to the film lies in its adoption of the ensemble disaster movie structure so popular in the 1970s. The premise is simple: take a very large cast, add a series of ever-escalating disasters, sit back and watch the resulting mayhem. In such films as *The Poseidon Adventure* (1972) or *The Towering Inferno* (1974) much of the entertainment was derived from the juxtaposition of big stars and big peril, not knowing who would make it to the end. Of course, in these films a few of the headliners survive and this is where *Mars Attacks!* pays huge comedy dividends - it is the little guys who pull through, not the big cheeses. The fun of not being indestructible is clear. After all, what actor doesn't relish a good death scene? Jack Nicholson even gets two deaths, giving balanced comedy performances that are easily his best since Ken Russell's *Tommy* (1975). As the President his role is finely tuned, recalling Peter Sellers' part(s) in Kubrick's *Dr Strangelove* (1964) especially in the war room sequences. Another loud person doomed to a nasty death is the Rude Gambler played by ex-Penguin Danny de Vito with deliberate irritability. All these characters have to vie for screen time so naturally are less than three-dimensional and work better for it - Nicholson's crass Vegas businessman keen for the Martian dollar, Bening's ex-alcoholic new age hippie seeking extraterrestrial salvation, Michael J Fox's long-suffering 'proper' reporter or Martin Short's sleazy publicist with an unhealthy libido. Amidst all this we find the most inspired cameo from Tom Jones, who not only gets to sing 'It's Not Unusual' twice but does so to adoring animals. This too is in the tradition of the lower end of the sci-fi/horror market where any teen idol would be hurriedly filmed to bolster sales. The fact that he pulls this off is a miracle in itself.

The heroes offer another example of the disenfranchised family. Both Richie and Taffy have their full complement of parents and, despite being totally opposite ends of the social divide, share a common bond. Richie's family reject him because he isn't a mindless patriot like his disturbing brother while, despite Taffy's upbringing, her feelings and concerns are ignored by her family. The dysfunctional families survive the ordeal, rather than end up victims. Sure, the Williams' house is all but demolished by the film's close but the family are back together again. Louise has proven to be a determined, fierce and good mother. The two kids have fought valiantly for their country. Big Byron has risen from the doldrums and single-handedly beaten a battalion of aliens in hand-to-hand combat.

The main focus of audience interest lies with the Martians themselves, mischievous imps whose sole purpose is to have fun. These are not the face-less alien masses of *Earth vs. Flying Saucers* (1956) or *War Of The Worlds* (1953) but animated characters whose mannerisms cause the viewer to smile rather than grimace. This can be gleaned from the opening, where the Warner's logo is infiltrated by a Martian flying saucer followed by a stam-pede of barbecuing cattle. When we first set eyes on a Martian it is via a broadcast interrupting television signals. This is filmed in exactly the same manner as the 'Criswell Predicts' opening of Ed Wood's *Plan 9 From Outer Space*. The little rascals read *Playboy*, perhaps in a nod to *Mars Needs Women* (1966), and later mock the world by inhaling a nuclear explosion as though it is helium. This is wish fulfilment at its fullest - the ultimate kickback against authority and conformity. The Martians are doing what they want, not what they are meant to. Yes, they are an evil disruptive influence that threatens our very survival but boy, do they know how to party. Like a cat playing with its food they are inventive in their curiosity and cruelty. Experiments on board their ship see them dissecting cows, clowns and even swapping the head of dippy fashion reporter Nathalie with her dog, although even in canine form she manages to continue her flirtatious relationship with Professor Kessler. The humans have no qualms about dissecting Martians, particularly Spy Girl with her NO_2 chewing gum, but at least wait until they are dead. As this is a major motion picture (*Dr Strangelove* bravely attempted the less commercial route by destroying the Earth) these anarchists must be defeated, and the aliens' denouement is as gory and ridiculous as any - the music of Slim Whit-man provides the ultimate weapon of mass destruction. The fact that the Mar-tians explode to Whitman is hardly surprising because it is such a hideous noise, but it is the preferred music of someone disenfranchised by society, in this case the old. Those who scoff at Whitman in place of reactionary C&W are just as conservative as those who hate Marilyn Manson - it's just a matter of perspective.

Style And Score: The film employs the stunning and vividly colourful cine-matography of DP Peter Suschitzky who is best known for his expressive low-key work on David Cronenberg's films, so in some ways he would seem to be an odd choice. Suschitzky's work on *Dead Ringers* was suitably lumi-nescent but his earlier work shows foundations of an even brighter colour pal-ette, specifically on the cult musical *The Rocky Horror Picture Show* (1975) and Ken Russell's hugely underrated biopic *Lisztomania* (1975). Despite the remit to make a film steeped in B-Movie aesthetics, the cost and detail of the effects work was suitably big budget. While the spaceships look "like a giant hubcap" (another reference to *Plan 9 From Outer Space*) and have structural similarities to the more upmarket *Forbidden Planet* (1956) or *The Day The Earth Stood Still* (1951, the pacifist answer to *Mars Attacks!*) they are nonetheless state-of-the-art, despite their retro look. This can also be seen in the title sequence where the alien spaceships take off from Mars and begin their voyage towards Earth. The planet, the ships and the formations are beautifully 1950s both in use of extreme Technicolor contrasts (Mars is as red as red can be) and in ship design and movement. They even have an almost imperceptible wobble. But count the number, look at the overlaid formations, marvel at the planetary detail (built to huge scale) and the expense is clear. Danny Elfman provides a pounding pulsating score with lots of whoops and Theramin-style sirens in the very mould of those classic movies.

Making Of: Key to the film's success lay in the way that the Martians were portrayed. Initially the intention was to use stop-frame animation blended with live action. Stop-motion is one of the most painstaking methods to realise properly, but the results are worth it. This is the technique used in *Nightmare Before Christmas* but here the models were to be integrated into live action, as pioneered by such effects geniuses as Willis O'Brien (*King Kong*, *Mighty Joe Young*) and Ray Harryhausen (*Seventh Voyage Of Sinbad*). In particular, Harryhausen's work on *Jason and the Argonauts* (1963), which has a renowned skeleton fight, was to define the way that the Martians would move - organic yet otherworldly. To this end Manchester-based Mackinnon & Saunders were hired to deal with the intricate stop-motion work, as well as supply life-sized Martians for set dressing and the autopsy scenes. It was agreed that the Martians should not be seen as men in rubber costumes. Models were made and each Martian head was cast with a number of different expressions, hand sculpted to show the various reactions required: angry, inquisitive, laughing etc. All the components were in place when the bombshell struck. At the last minute Burton decided that stop-motion, while creating the look necessary to give the picture an authentic period feel, was too risky and time-consuming. A problem with mega-buck pictures is that they have cash to throw at a project but not time. Naturally Mackinnon & Saunders were more than a touch disappointed with the decision but their work is still evident in the final film. Accurate measurements and details from the models were sent over to the new effects company on board: ILM.

ILM (Industrial Light and Magic) took the model data and used this, and the hand-painted colour work to render the intergalactic imps as CGI models. Thus the production had gone from traditional methods to those relatively recent, accentuating the ethos of having complete aesthetic control to convey the impression of schlock. It could so easily have gone wrong and denied the film any charm (CGI is notoriously difficult to emote) but fortunately ILM stuck to the remit and the Martians bounce around with manic glee and betray occasional jerkiness of movement. It is quite an achievement because it does manage to maintain the balance between slick and retro.

Background: There have been many bizarre licenses in the history of Hollywood. We've had cartoon spin-offs (*Popeye*), comic adaptations (*Superman, Batman*), computer games (*Super Mario Brothers*) and even 19th-Century literature (*Sense And Sensibility*). Surely though *Mars Attacks!* beats the lot because it is based on a series of bubble-gum cards. Topps are a modern American institution, bringing the concept of trading cards to the nation's youth with football and baseball statistics. It's not all sports though, because in 1962 they launched a new series: *Mars Attacks!* - a set of 55 lurid colour cards depicting alien atrocities. The level of gore was extreme at the time but not without precedent - a previous series of Topps cards about the American Civil War was similarly brutal, but justified as history. The *Mars Attacks!* cards revelled in schlock versions of HG Wells' *War Of The Worlds* with sensationalist descriptions as people were crushed and maimed. Despite the slaughter of so many humans, the most notorious card remained Number 36: Destroying A Dog where a wailing child pleads to no avail as a Martian warrior blows his pet pooch away. When the protests became too noisy the cards were withdrawn and have since become collectors' items. Burton remembered these vaguely from his youth and, with Jonathan Gems, set about bringing them to the big screen. They had met previously when *Batman* was in production and began working on another screen version of *The Fall Of The House Of Usher* by Edgar Allan Poe, a perennial favourite with the early surrealist directors, Eastern European animators and Roger Corman. Sadly that project fell through but the colour, opulence and style of Corman's film carried forward into *Mars Attacks!*.

Trivia: Mars Attacks! is the first Burton feature film that doesn't incorporate the main character's name in the title.

The Aftermath: Mars Attacks! was not a success. Unfortunately many people didn't get the joke and, despite saturation advertising campaigns and some of the coolest tie-in merchandising ever, the result was a financial flop.

The Verdict: 5/5

Tackling The Classics Head On

"Eliminate the impossible and whatever remains, no matter how improbable, must be the truth."

Arthur Conan Doyle

Sleepy Hollow was a long time coming after *Mars Attacks!* and for good reason - it was not originally going to be Burton's follow-up to the gleeful black comedy. Instead Burton spent about a year working on *Superman Lives!*. Superman was always seen as DC's rival character to Batman. He had enjoyed a number of incarnations both on film and television. *Superman* (1978) was the blockbuster of its year while the TV series *The New Adventures Of Superman* continued to be popular well into the 1990s. With the guy who made *Batman* such a smash, what could go wrong? *Superman Lives!* had spent a long time not getting onto the screen. Various scriptwriters were involved with the project, notably *Clerks* writer/director Kevin Smith whose screenplay was first rejected as being too expensive to make (ironic since Smith, a lifelong comic fanatic, has made a number of popular films for virtually peanuts) and then by Burton as being unsuitable. After a long gestating time Warner Brothers pulled the plug on the project, getting concerned that the necessarily monumental budget would be difficult to recoup at the box office. Fortunately for Burton he had a 'pay or play' deal, which meant that he got his fee regardless of whether the film actually went into production. However with *Superman Lives!* effectively dead, Burton turned to *Sleepy Hollow*. The screenplay was penned by Andrew Kevin Walker who had written David Fincher's gloomathon serial-killer film *Se7en* (1995). Walker was clearly an aficionado for the same kind of horror films that Burton loved. *Se7en* was based, for all its noir overtones and total absence of kitsch tongue-in-cheek Grand Guignol, on the Vincent Price *Dr Phibes* films (*The Abominable Dr Phibes* (1971) and *Dr Phibes Rises Again* (1972)) and the hysterical black comedy *Theater Of Blood* (1972). For *Sleepy Hollow* though, the influence would turn to another British horror institution: Hammer films.

Sleepy Hollow (1999)

Crew: Dir: Tim Burton, Prd: Scott Rudin, Adam Schroeder, Co-Prd: Kevin Yagher, Exec Prd: Francis Ford Coppola, Larry Franco, Story: Andrew Kevin Walker, Kevin Yagher, Scr: Andrew Kevin Walker, DP: Emmanuel Lubezki, Music: Danny Elfman, 100 mins

Cast: Johnny Depp (Ichabod Crane), Christina Richie (Katrina Van Tassel), Christopher Lee (Burgomaster), Miranda Richardson (Lady Van Tassel), Michael Gambon (Baltus Van Tassel), Lisa Marie (Ichabod's Mother), Richard Griffiths (Magistrate Philipse), Casper Van Dien (Brom Van Brunt), Christopher Walken (Hessian Horseman), Jeffrey Jones (Reverend Steenwyck), Michael Gough (Notary James Hardenbrook)

Plot: Twenty years ago a Hessian mercenary plied his bloody trade in the vicinity of Sleepy Hollow. He carved a path of limbs and heads before meeting a similar fate, dumped in an unmarked grave, his face frozen in a wide-eyed grimace, his yellow filed teeth mockingly defiant. His legacy remains, instilled deep in the psyche of the local community as the Headless Horseman, a relentless decapitator on his jet black steed. Rural superstition? You'd think so. But with three executions in the last week, all found with missing heads, even if the tales are fanciful they surely warrant some scrutiny. This is where stern-faced rationalist Ichabod Crane comes in. Crane may well be a city boy, unused to the ways of the isolated community but he has a remit to get to the bottom of the brutal murders. If he doesn't, his already sullied reputation as a meddling crank will take a further turn for the worse, for the authorities are unprepared to embrace the full magnitude of deductive scientific reason. Ichabod must prove himself.

Arriving at Sleepy Hollow he sets straight to work, residing in the home of the affluent Van Tassels he becomes drawn to their daughter Katrina. When a local man, Masbath, becomes victim number four (his son adopted by Ichabod as an assistant) he realises desperate measures are called for, especially when given a surreptitious tip-off that the unfortunate Masbath was actually the fifth casualty in the mysterious beheadings. Sure enough autopsies on the exhumed bodies reveal that a previous victim, Emily Winship, had been with child and the horseman had claimed that life also. Crane's rigid belief in the human origin of the murders is soon shattered when he witnesses the gruesome beheading of a very frightened Magistrate Philipse. It seems as though nothing can stop the tide of atrocities affecting the little village. Matters are not helped by the community scallywags playing ghoulish jokes on Ichabod. One such individual is Brom but he has special reason to dislike the outsider - he has been courting the fair Katrina. Still, any real concerns about rivalry are swiftly curtailed, for Brom becomes another ex-villager, torn asunder in front of Ichabod's very eyes after the horseman has performed a particularly nasty hat-trick of assassinations on the family of the local midwife.

Despite Ichabod's initial scepticism regarding events, he is now utterly convinced that the spectre is real, deadly and has a purpose ("The horseman does not kill at random"). This last conclusion came with Brom's death - the horseman did not care for the headstrong farmer's boy until provoked into battle. It could mean only one thing - the horseman is controlled by someone who has something very dear to him... his head. Ichabod, young Masbath and Katrina, assisted by a prophetic woodland witch, find the Tree of Pain at the end of the Indian Trail, the final resting place of the Hessian rider. They see the tree spew blood instead of sap. They see the missing heads in its roots. They see the ferocious cranially-deficient equestrian ride forth from the bowels of the Earth, his mighty steed scattering forest debris in its wake, doggedly focused on the next terrible assignment. Accepting the supernatural should not have been difficult for Ichabod, as his mother was a witch, tortured to death in the name of saving her soul. Katrina's deceased mother was also one, but Katrina embraced her mother's esoteric ways and engages in arcane practices - a trait that Ichabod is reticent about condoning, especially when he discovers glyphs etched in purple chalk under his bed.

What has this to do with Van Garrett's Last Will and Testament? Why is Lady Van Tassel engaging in amorous nocturnal encounters? It all becomes too much for Ichabod... Baltus Van Tassel meets a horrible end at a public meeting, Katrina is incensed with Ichabod's blinkered reliance on logic, and even Lady Van Tassel appears to have come a cropper whilst picking arrowroot - her nibblesome neck neatly knocked in two by the horseman's searing blade. Time to leave. But wait! Are things really as they seem? Could Katrina be a good witch and not a bad one? And what if the deceased are not as dead as they seem?

Comment: Burton's assertion of *Sleepy Hollow* is that "It felt good... to feel like you're making a Hammer horror film." This gives key indications to the film's aesthetic direction and provides understanding as to why, suddenly, he decided to make a period horror film. Although is has British horror sensibilities, it is based firmly in American literature. The emphasis is to evoke the nostalgia of the sort of films Burton enjoyed as a child, not necessarily to recreate them. Hammer films have had a bit of a renaissance in recent years and are generally seen as quaint exploitation. Partly this is down to the fact that the majority of the macabre and supernatural happenings were founded in a distant past or distant climes (normally somewhere in Eastern Europe). This enabled them to be viewed more sympathetically by the censor's hands, allowing more sex and blood than was normally permitted for a British film because it was in some way 'heritage' gore. Hammer further managed to detach themselves from the more lurid end of the market by telling adult faerie tales. *Sleepy Hollow* is in just such a tradition. It gets away with quite savage violence because the threat is purely fantastical. Indeed it warranted no more than a 15 rating in the UK, a sign that for all its decapitations, witchcraft and autopsies, it is ultimately harmless.

Despite the fantastical slant there are many horrors that go decidedly beyond the pale, but these are generally not depicted explicitly. Two scenes in particular stand out by their implication. When the midwife's family are slaughtered we see the horseman kill the husband directly before descending upon the screaming wife, while phantasmagorical projections emanating from their child's lamp spin around the room. The young boy cowers beneath the floorboards as the horseman decapitates his mother off screen. But her head drops onto the floor and cold eyes stare at him through the gaps in the wood. This is disturbing enough, but the horseman returns to complete his task, smashing the floorboards to capture the child. The only indication that he has taken the child's life is in the slight tightening of his headbag. The scene, for all its implied horror, is indicative of the kind of violence that's acceptable towards which kind of person. The other implied horror sequence occurs when Ichabod discovers the fifth victim and performs his first autopsy. The implication from the sword wound in the belly of the pregnant Winship is that the Horseman also decapitated her foetus. There are exceptions to this however, with some scenes being designed to confront and shock. Of particular note is the iron maiden sequence when Ichabod remembers the origin of the marks on his hands as he discovers the fate of his mother. The iron maiden slowly opens and out flops his mother, gushing oceans of blood. In post-production Burton decided that the scene seriously lacked gore and extensive CGI work was required to add the missing viscera.

One scene that is straight out of Hammer is the climactic windmill fight. Although many have commented on its similarity to the closing of James Whale's *Frankenstein* (as it is), the dynamics, lighting and pace are straight from the exhilarating climax of Terence Fisher's *Brides Of Dracula* (1960) as Peter Cushing battles against Baron Meinster culminating in a scramble down the sails and, in this case, an end to a vampire's curse. Ichabod's character is ostensibly based on a rationalising form of Hammer's van Helsing, so memorably played by Cushing, but there are significant differences which also give *Sleepy Hollow* much of its humour. The main point is that, unlike van Helsing, Ichabod is wrong. His demeanour approaches Cushing's portrayal and his tasks are similarly macabre, but no matter how much Ichabod tries to exhibit the sang froid of a scientist, he recoils at any atrocity with patent queasiness and unease. Such is his squeamishness that he faints on a number of occasions, winces visibly every time he is doused in blood and cringes at the sight of a spider!

The film plays a great deal with the rational and the fantastical, with Ichabod's character defining the dichotomy. He denies the existence of the supernatural, but perhaps it is because he could never follow in mummy's footsteps and squeeze the lifeblood out of bats or chop off ravens' claws. Yet his concepts of deductive reasoning and the evolution of forensic science verged on heresy for the time. He is sent by the authorities to solve the crimes not so that he can prove his theories, but so he can fail. Finding the area (as in Irving's story) awash with superstition and deep-rooted belief in witchcraft, his openminded attitude in the city becomes blinkered. "You are bewitched by reason" - "I am beaten down by it." It is also a reflection on his childhood trauma.

Style And Score: Visually there are many similarities to *The Nightmare Before Christmas*. The film opens with a pursuit through the cornfields ending with a murder in front of a pumpkin-headed scarecrow, that becomes daubed with the blood. These pumpkin jack-o'-lanterns are in many of the external scenes, but the spirit of Jack Skellington extends further than that. The Tree of Pain is described by Ichabod as "a bridge between two worlds" rather like the forest trees. Then there is the snow. Here the story begins and ends chronologically with snow - the Hessian rider's tale is set in winter and Ichabod's return to New York is heralded by snow. This later shot (the last in the film) indicates that Sleepy Hollow's twenty-year autumn is over and that winter (always a season for aesthetic joy) is here. The daytime colour palette is definitely autumnal, with muted colours, misty fields and bare, barren trees in the forest.

Burton describes Depp's performance as of a "silent star quality" and this extends to the rest of the cast. This is not to say it is stagy but rather expressionistic, where the looks and actions convey the meaning. The film is set two hundred years in the past so this approach gives the characterisation a quality that 'feels' like the time. To emphasise this, the instruments used by Ichabod look as though they could have been contemporaneous but, as with other Burton films, this is an otherwhen, a time outside of normal history. Ichabod's instruments look closer to torture devices than scientific gadgets, but their detail makes them fascinating with a resemblance to the devices designed by the Mantle brothers in Cronenberg's *Dead Ringers* (1988) and the eyepieces recall the steam-punk costumes of Jeunet and Caro's *City Of Lost Children* (1995).

Making Of: In realising *Sleepy Hollow* Burton travelled to England. Partly this was due to the suitability of the countryside to reflect an idealised upper state New York (and the weather, ideal for muted browns and overcast lighting...) and partly because a large portion of the cast were British thespians, many of them performing rep in the evenings after shooting had wrapped for the day. The sight of respected British actors hanging up their severed heads after a long day's decapitation to play Shakespeare was something that partic-

72

ularly amused Burton. The heads themselves were painstakingly realised by Kevin Yagher Productions (it was Yagher who suggested the story of *Sleepy Hollow*) and each was carefully moulded from the actors' features with every piece of hair or stubble woven into the resulting cast by hand. For the scene where Magistrate Philipse is decapitated such that his head spins atop his neck before toppling to the floor, a fully armatured body was built to crumple after the blow.

The carriage chase towards the climax took three weeks to film. Like most of the movie, it was shot indoors on soundstages. Although this method creates some problems (not least of which are galloping horses in a closed environment) and can be more expensive, it gave Burton greater control over the lighting and colour matching. It also meant that the forest could be populated by dead trees, giving it a further eerie edge. Full soundstage shooting for external locations is nothing new, but its use in this context (tracking action suspense) has its roots in the Jacques Tourneur/Val Lewton classic *Cat People* (1942).

Although the headless horseman is the raison d'être for the tale, Christopher Walken generally only played the character with head intact. This is not to say he got off lightly as his scenes were very physical and required him to wear excruciating contact lenses and teeth fittings. And then there were the horses. Being a city lad, Christopher was not too comfortable with the beasts. A pity because he had to spend some time looking as though he was proficient with them. That Johnny Depp was not too hot either didn't matter - his character was meant to look uncomfortable. One of the solutions was to use a mechanical horse for some of the close-ups – they found the one originally used by Elizabeth Taylor on *National Velvet* (1944), and it still worked! However, when it came to wielding axe and sword Ray Park took the swordsman's role. He also played Darth Maul in *The Phantom Menace* (1999) and Toad in *X-Men* (2000). How did they get him to look like Christopher Walken? By making him wear the same costume and hiding his face - a similar technique to the Tom the Chiropractor/Bela Lugosi substitution in *Plan 9 From Outer Space*. The difference between that classic switch and this one is that here they didn't just hide the face (similar ears or no) but took it off completely by blue screening a hood and digitally painting in the background. The result? A genuine-looking headless horseman.

Background: Washington Irving's *The Legend Of Sleepy Hollow* is one of the stalwarts of 18th-Century American literature and is still enjoyed to this day. The reason for this lies in its reader-friendly length and spooky campfire-tale style that epitomise the traditional horror story. Irving's tale is a simple one... Ichabod Crane, a well-educated man, makes his living in a Dutch farming community by teaching the children. Paid by donations, he lives by simple means, wandering from home to home. Being educated in the ways of etiquette and possessing hands unsullied by hard labour, he is a big hit with the ladies and often the topic of gossip, which he peddles to great reward. He is a superstitious man, steeped heavily in the legends and lore of the area's witch-craft and black arts. But the community is situated near Sleepy Hollow, home of the headless horseman. One night, after Crane has tried to woo the hand of the rich and daring (she wears dresses where you can occasionally glimpse her ankles - hussy!) Katrina Von Tassel at a dance party he has the unfortu-nate pleasure of confronting the Headless horseman...

The Legend of Sleepy Hollow had been filmed before, most notably in an animated version by Disney that stayed fairly faithful to the story. In Burton's film some of the names of the characters and settings have remained, but the tale is more of a springboard from which a new story can be told. Irving's eponymous hero Ichabod Crane has undergone a significant transformation in his cinematic interpretation. He is no longer a schoolteacher, no longer seeks work and certainly doesn't engage in minor farm chores to endear himself to the community. Most significantly, the new Ichabod is no longer an expert on the occult but is a man of uncommon science and reason - a precursor for deductive methods and forensic expertise.

Trivia: Apparently one of the most difficult aspects of the shoot involved finding a Cardinal (a red bird, not a member of the Catholic church) in Brit-ain. "There is one Cardinal in Britain, and we couldn't use it." One suggestion offered for this unusual problem was to use a pigeon, and paint it red! In the end the metaphor of the bird and its cage, the optical trick given to Ichabod by his mother and the illusory nature of freedom, meant that its place in the nar-rative was crucial. Rick Heinrichs won an Oscar for his superb art direction.

The Verdict: 5/5

Monkey Business

The road to Tim Burton's *Planet Of The Apes* was not an easy one and he was far from first choice for the film. Plans for a new Apes film began in 1993 when Oliver Stone was mooted to helm the project either as director, producer or both. Matters escalated as a series of directors and scriptwriters joined and left the project. Thus we could have faced the prospect of Chris Columbus, James Cameron, Peter Hyams or even Phillip Noyce in the director's chair. All of these fell through until Fox were left with Frank Darabont or Tim Burton. Following the success of *Sleepy Hollow* Fox plumped for Burton, but even then the journey from script to screen was not easy. Already the basis of the film had changed substantially over the preceding years and, whilst William Broyles' screenplay *The Visitor* (the film's working title) was favourably received, it was deemed far too expensive to film, necessitating a flurry of additional rewrites to bring the budget down to a manageable(!) $100 million.

Planet Of The Apes (2001)

Crew: Dir: Tim Burton, Prd: Richard D Zanuck, Scr: William Broyles Jr., Lawrence Konner, Mark D Rosenthal from a novel by Pierre Boulle, DP: Philippe Rousselot, Music: Danny Elfman, Production Design: Rick Heinrichs, 120 mins

Cast: Mark Wahlberg (Capt. Leo Davidson), Estella Warren (Daena), Tim Roth (Thade), Helena Bonham Carter (Ari), Michael Clarke Duncan (Colonel Attar), Paul Giamatti (Limbo), David Warner (Sandar), Kris Kristofferson (Karubi), Lisa Marie (Nova), Rick Baker (Old Ape No. 2), Charlton Heston (Thade's father)

Plot: Leo Davidson has worked with monkeys for most of his life - both literally and figuratively. Up on the Oberon Space Station he conducts experiments to improve the co-ordination and intelligence of our simian brethren to facilitate safer deep-space travel. His colleagues however are not so convinced as to the humanity inherent in his charges and treat the monkeys less like monkeys and more like, well, guinea pigs. Following a strange electromagnetic storm beaming television signals back from a distant galaxy, Davidson's finest subject, a chimpanzee, is sent on an exploratory mission in pod Alpha, human life being too important to risk. Davidson's chagrin at this inhumane attitude is reflected in his decision to follow his fur-covered protégé in pod Delta ("I'm gonna get my chimp - never send in a monkey to do a man's job"). Big mistake. Davidson's rescue mission goes banana shaped and he is flung far into the future (it's a relativity thing) and far into space, landing on alien soil...

...well actually not so much landing on alien soil and more like crashing headlong into an alien lake, effectively taking his capsule out and forcing him to seek land rapidly. Once there he encounters a tribe of humans being pursued by a marauding band of ape militia. This, needless to say, bemuses the good captain. Captured with the rest of the humans he is carted off to the apes' city where his suspicions are confirmed - this is a world where humans are subservient and intellectually bereft, and the various breeds of ape rule the planet. Not all apes are quite so species-ist though - the Senator's daughter Ari has been a devout human rights activist since she was a little girl and recognises Davidson's intelligence almost instantly. She is not alone. Her potential suitor, the megalomaniac monkey militiaman Thade, also singles out the extraterrestrial as worthy of attention but for entirely different and not so wholesome reasons. It is imperative therefore that the plucky humans escape their tree-clambering captors and try to make a new life outside the tyrannical rule of the apes. For Davidson an extra bonus would be to escape the planet altogether, preferably without one of the painful looking brandings that the apes seem so keen on dishing out.

As chance would have it, once they have escaped the confines of their immediate captivity they spot a signal on Davidson's portable communication device, a signal that means the space station Oberon is online and presumably still searching for the errant Captain. The signal emanates from the Forbidden Area, a part of the planet that is off-bounds to humans and is the sacred source of the apes' creation. There is nothing to lose as our intrepid band of apes and humans scurry their way to the evolutionary foundation of ape supremacy and their own uncertain destiny...

Comment: In many respects *Planet Of The Apes* seems to be a studio response to how *Mars Attacks!* should have been made - subdued, with earnestness and virtually lacking in overt humour. This is not to say that it lacks the characteristics that have become synonymous with Burton's oeuvre but rather that these elements are very much underplayed in the finished film. Were it not for Danny Elfman's marvellously percussive score and some occasionally striking design work from Rick Heinrichs you may well discover that you're simply seated in an above average summer blockbuster.

Many of Burton's themes are present in *Planet Of The Apes*, but they are not pushed to the fore. Ari is the intelligent daughter of the Senator (like Taffy in *Mars Attacks!*). She has opinions that she is not afraid to voice and has been active in human rights since childhood. When Leo explains the concept of the zoo to Ari, she is shocked and considers that apes on earth "choose not to talk, given the way you treat them." *Planet Of The Apes* also adheres to the Burton love of the outsider with Captain Davidson who, despite being a clean cut, all-American hero, is the extraterrestrial in a world he doesn't understand and which doesn't understand him. The fact that he is essentially dull compared to any of Burton's other protagonists is exactly the point - the twisted world sees not just a reversal of contemporary evolutionary hierarchy but also of the definition of the outsider. Additionally, the apes themselves are beyond our perception of a dominant species and, while this gives Burton the opportunity to ridicule human traits by having them parodied (notably in the instance where a card shark reveals that he has a card up his third sleeve causing his opponent to yell "Cheater," recalling Tarzan's cheeky monkey Cheetah), it is clear that the apes provide far more fascination than their human counterparts and become the misunderstood monsters of the story. They offer all the foibles we recognise in humanity but their traits are augmented due to their superior dexterity - ape guitarists can simultaneously tap and strum, Ari can write with her feet while her hands are otherwise occupied, and they all have wide-ranging emotions and desires. Indeed, despite the humans' prodigious speaking abilities (after a period of muteness early on you can't shut them up) they are resolutely bland and vacant - even Davidson suffers from this to some extent. You empathise almost entirely with the apes. By the time Davidson is prepared to leave for Earth, he has helped the humans rebel and created the template for a society where apes and humans can coexist as equals, but he has only really forged a bond with Ari. It then comes as some surprise when Daena gives him a huge kiss, because at this point you are expecting any form of emotional interaction to come from Ari. Indeed one persistent rumour that had been mooted since the film first started shooting is a more physical encounter between ape and man, a scene that comically almost happens in the book (if only he wasn't so unattractive!) and seems suited to the film. For whatever reason (it is asserted that the scene is just a hangover from a previous screenplay) we don't get to see any ape on human action.

Strangely despite the book's emphasis on human experimentation and its parallels with animal experiments on Earth, Burton's film only contains fleeting references to this aspect of the story. This is a pity because it would have been a golden opportunity to resurrect the mad scientist/Vincent Price theme that pervades most of his other work. The closest we get is the helpful advice "Wear your gloves when you have to handle humans," an analogy connecting them with disease.

The final fight seems half-hearted, but perhaps this was intended. We've been shown the extent of the apes' dominance and contempt for the human race but also their well-founded fears of human intelligence. Thade's dying father (played by Charlton Heston) realises, as all the apes do, that if the humans harness technology then any hopes of continued ape dominance are shattered. "Their ingenuity goes hand in hand with their cruelty." The extent of the humans' almost pathological need for destruction is illustrated when Ari, who helped them escape and risked her life for them, reveals the apes' fear of water to Daena. Daena's response? "That's why we pray for rain," as she looks with utter hatred at her saviour. In the battle, only the first wave of the ape army is sent to attack the humans, which is decimated by the Oberon's last drops of fuel and brute strength. The apes capitulate because they do not know the technology that wiped out their troops and that this phenomenon cannot be repeated. It is far better for them to live together as equals and not evoke any further wrath. As they bury the bodies the union is confirmed: "They will be mourned together, as it should be from now on."

The original *Planet Of The Apes* film ends memorably with the discovery of the Statue of Liberty half buried in the beach and Burton takes the opportunity to play with this most poignant of 60s images. When his party goes to the Forbidden Area and comes across the remains of Davidson's space station, the way it is initially shot recalls the spike-rimmed head of the Statue of Liberty (and also, curiously, Gaudi's Sagrada Familia). Later, at the very close of the film when Leo has returned to Earth he crashes through America's National Mall, past the Washington Monument and finds himself at the foot of the Lincoln Memorial - only now simian features stare down upon our despondent traveller. This is a similar return to home that faced the protagonist in Boulle's original novel (albeit in Paris) although the desecration of a respected national monument into alien form comes straight from the Martian improvement of Mount Rushmore in *Mars Attacks!*.

Style and Score: Visually, of all Burton's films this somehow feels the least 'Burtonesque' and perhaps the most disappointing aspect of *Planet Of The Apes* is the cinematography. At individual moments (for example the battle scenes where the background is veiled with dust, the warning effigies on the edge of the Forbidden Area or the crimson tents of the apes' camp) we are shown classic Burton iconography, but generally the colours are so muted and grainy that you wonder why they bothered. The backdrops are dull and the overall look rejects contrast in favour of a dank, leaden landscape of depression and misery. Burton is associated with dark or Gothic countenance but here there is a rejection of contrast or interest, with only the aforementioned tents providing any real focus. Danny Elfman was under a good deal of pressure to write the score, as the film was still being completed while he was composing! It's another great soundtrack, very rhythmic and tribal with a variety of percussion instruments dominating the proceedings. It is totally in tune with the lack of technology on the planet and blends perfectly with this aspect of the film's ethos that "The smarter we get the more dangerous our world becomes" - the Burton concept of 'feeling' a film rather than analysing it.

Making Of: Much of *Planet Of The Apes* relies on updated versions of traditional effects rather than creating everything in a CGI environment. Many of the stunts and riding work were performed by the actors themselves for greater realism, although obviously the more dangerous or specialised stunt work was body-doubled. However, the stars of the film are clearly the apes, who blow the humans away in terms of screen personae. Make-up supremo

Rick Baker was the man responsible for the remarkable ape masks and had only three months to create 500 apes of varying degrees of complexity. In addition to the exemplary make-up work, the actors' movements were choreographed to get the impression of ape-ishness. Terry Notary, ex-*Cirque Du Soleil*, helped the actors get in touch with their 'inner ape' and mimic the movements of our ancestors in a way that makes the film seem believably simian. This even included training the extras in the background to imitate monkey mannerisms. The results are no more apparent than during the final battle when the first wave of ape troops descend upon the primitives – on all fours and galloping in an entirely convincing manner.

One major problem facing the film was the speed with which it was necessary to make it. It went into production in November 2000 with a firm release date of July 2001. As scriptwriter Mark Rosenthal commented, "For this movie, everybody jumped off a cliff and on the way down we figured out what it should be." (*SFX: Planet Of The Apes Special 2001*)

Background: The original film version of *Planet Of The Apes* (1967, directed by Franklin J Schaffner) was one of Hollywood's more successful attempts to make a thought-provoking science fiction film that also had the action and adventure that audiences crave. It's a strange mix of space travel gone wrong, humour, evolution, a critique on race/class issues and it even finds time for a touch of romance. Although a little heavy-handed it is a solid two hours of entertainment by anyone's standards. It works even today, thanks to the astonishing make-up (John Chambers quite rightly won a special Oscar for his team's outstanding work) and, of course, the downplayed shock ending. Not only was the film a critical success but a commercial one, spawning a plethora of (increasingly inferior) sequels (*Beneath* (1970), *Escape* (1971), *Conquest* (1972), *Battle* (1973)), television series, books, toys and comics. The original film was based on a series of stories by Pierre Boulle (whose most famous work remains the non-genre *Bridge On The River Kwai* filmed by David Lean in 1957), the first of which *La Planète Des Singes* provided the loose basis of the film. Although the film lacks the discourse and irony of the novel it is nonetheless one of the more interesting mainstream films of the 60s. The main points of departure from the book are that the film is set entirely on Earth as shown by the Statue of Liberty climax (the book sees a return to Earth where the Eiffel Tower is still intact but the apes are in control) and the technological capabilities of the apes are far more advanced in the book. The franchise provided healthy returns with a substantial amount of income generated from merchandise tie-ins of the sort that seem very familiar to a post-*Star Wars* consumer.

Trivia: Planet Of The Apes was being completed right up to the line to the extent that studio executives only saw the completed film days before it was due to premiere. "The first time they showed me the poster and on the bottom it said: 'This film has not yet been rated," Burton said. "I said why not be accurate and say 'This film has not yet been shot'?" (*The Guardian*, August 3, 2001) Eventually the film opened as planned. The initial weekend's grosses broke all non-holiday records (although the record was held for a week and superseded by *Rush Hour 2*) and exceeded its budget within a fortnight. For Burton this means another palpable hit and a continuation of his A-list status. Unfortunately, it also means that in the future he will have further tough fights for artistic control because the Hollywood factory is becoming increasingly franchise-based.

Planet Of The Apes is a fine film when viewed alongside the standard pop-corn-munching fare that a summer blockbuster is expected to provide, but as a Tim Burton film it lies marginally above *Batman* in the evolutionary scale, rather as monkeys do humans...

The Verdict: 3/5

Other Skellingtons In The Closet - Burton As Producer

Family Dog (1987-1993)

Crew: Prd: Tim Burton, Steven Spielberg, Dennis Klein, Music: Danny Elfman with additional music by Steve Bartek

Plot: Take one selfish family who blatantly ignore the attentions of their pet. Make said pet a touch of a scallywag. Blend. Watch as ensuing mayhem and japes occur before your very eyes.

Comment: *Family Dog* was originally broadcast as a one-off animation in 1987 as part of Steven Spielberg's *Amazing Stories* and proved successful in its offbeat character designs and humour. With Burton becoming hot property after *Batman* and *Beetlejuice,* a series based upon the characters was green lighted for Spielberg's Amblin Entertainment. With Burton and Spielberg as executive producers (as well as Dennis Klein who provided most of the stories and scripts) it was felt that it would naturally be instantly successful. On top of that, the original cartoon had the involvement of Brad Bird, a friend from Burton's days at Disney who later worked on such classics as *The Simpsons*. Danny Elfman and Steve Bartek provided the music. Unfortunately only ten episodes were made and broadcast. Only the *Amazing Stories* pilot was ever available on video in the UK (and long since deleted) but the series can still be obtained on NTSC in the States where it is currently enjoying a (very) small renaissance. Not as bad as might be expected for a TV show, but expectations were high and merely average was presumably not good enough.

The Nightmare Before Christmas (1993)

Crew: Dir: Henry Selick, Prd: Tim Burton, Denise Di Novi, Scr: Caroline Thompson, Music, Lyrics and Score: Danny Elfman, Visual Consultant: Rick Heinrichs, 76 mins

Cast: Danny Elfman, Chris Sarandon, Paul Reubens, Catherine O'Hara

Plot: Jack Skellington, the Pumpkin King, is having a bit of a mid-death crisis. Despite his position as guiding figurehead of Halloweentown, he feels that there is something missing. A chance discovery of a door in a tree in a secret glade in a spooky forest leads Jack into a new world of colour, snow, happy faces and the spirit of Christmas. Perhaps this holds the key to his misanthropy. Inspired, he gets straight to work, trying to distil the essence of Christmas in his laboratory, much to the concern of the townsfolk. Jack plans to be the next Santa and distribute all the lovely presents he has made for the good little boys and girls. However his idea of nice toys doesn't quite agree with popular opinion, as the children find out on Christmas morning when their gifts of dolls and train sets have become giant snakes or a gruesome severed head. But his esteem reaches an all-time low when his philanthropy is met with hostility. He and his skeletal reindeer are shot down by considerable artillery fire. Dejected, the only things that can help him are the restoration of normality in his world and true love, which is where the delightful but detachable Sally comes in.

"It is more beautiful than I imagined it would be, thanks to Henry and his talented crew of artists, animators, and designers."

Tim Burton, *The Film, The Art, The Vision*

"I'm more upset about how much credit Tim Burton received on *The Nightmare Before Christmas...* I think his contributions cannot be denied. But I was the guy who made the film for close on three years of my life."

Henry Selick, *Projections 5*

Comment: This delightful telling of Burton's poem remains the pinnacle of commercial animation. Despite the title *Tim Burton's Nightmare Before Christmas,* is not a Burton film, it is a Henry Selick one, yet it looks and feels far more Burtonesque than these facts would suggest. This boils down to the characters created from Burton's original drawings and the sets - almost as though a Tim Burton film is designed rather than directed. It's also a timeless musical masterpiece that manages the rare feat of being both romantic and macabre. Danny Elfman composed the outstanding soundtrack that really lifts the film, and even sings all the Jack Skellington parts, providing the finest set of singalong numbers to grace a modern musical. Burton's themes are evident throughout: the misunderstood outsider who is basically good but rejected by so-called respectable society, and the love of the Gothic. Once again, there are very few evil creatures in the whole of Halloweentown. Only the Boogeyman and Sally's cruel creator represent genuine threats. Everyone else is basically decent, if grotesque. Far less likeable is Santa Claus himself - a rude, pompous, self-centred bore whose bright red clothes are at odds with his humourless personality. At least Jack wants to spread happiness. You get the distinct impression that Santa is just doing it because that's his job. The characters' design is nothing short of astonishing. All are given equal care and attention: the monster band that accompanies the soul-searching moonlit numbers, the swivel-headed jittery major, the bug-filled Boogeyman, the three mischievous double-crossing Santa-nappers Lock, Shock and Barrel.

Surprisingly for what is basically a children's film there is hardly a scene that goes by without something gross or disgusting happening, but it is all handled in such a gleeful manner that it never offends - besides, kids like gross. A modern classic that will continue to entertain and delight many years after current flavours of the month have been forgotten.

Making Of: The Nightmare Before Christmas was actually conceived while Burton was working at Disney ten years previously. The idea of creating a feature-length film using stop-frame animation was not new but examples are rare due to the immense time required and the considerable expense (other examples include Ladislaw Starewicz's *Tale Of The Fox* (1931) and Jiri Barta's *Pied Piper* (1985)). Disney invested a large sum into the picture and treated it in a 'hands off' manner which allowed the more grotesque elements of the (animated) cast to pass through unscathed. In Burton's original illustrated poem there were but three characters (Jack, Zero and Santa - although the denizens of Halloweentown and Christmas Town are described collectively) so when the film got the go-ahead for production the concepts were ready, but needed fleshing out. The collaboration between all the artists involved was quite complex. Danny Elfman composed all the songs using Burton's sketches as a basis for character development and Caroline Thompson used these to form the script. Henry Selick had the monumental task of pulling it all together as well as co-ordinating the entire production process. Technically this was a hugely ambitious project and key to Selick's ability as an animator lay in his enthusiasm for mixing media (cut-out, live, cel and model work) to produce a fantastical view on the world. *The Nightmare Before Christmas* shows the benefits of relying on old school stop-frame combined with state-of-the-art computer tracking (the camera swirls and glides like a Gene Kelly musical). The results are a perfect blend of the old and new - charming and timeless. The models are incredibly complex, each needing armatures, costumes and facial expressions. Indeed over 200 puppets were used in the film. The main centre of attention though remains Jack, a real labour of love - each perfectly lip-synched mouth movement made from a separate moulded head.

The Verdict: 5/5

Cabin Boy (1994)

Crew: Dir: Adam Resnick, Prd: Denise Di Novi, Tim Burton, Scr: Chris Elliot, Adam Resnick, Music: Steve Bartek, 80 mins

Cast: Chris Elliot, Russ Tamblyn, Ricki Lake

Plot: School's out for ever! Nathaniel, spoilt rude rich kid with the comedy essential ill-fitting trousers, contemptuously departs from his meagre academic career to help run his father's hotel chain in sunny Hawaii. However, Nathaniel's failure to recognise the vitriol his inappropriate aristocratic outbursts inflame in fellow human beings leads him to board The Filthy Whore - a smelly fishing vessel on a three-month net 'n' gut excursion – instead of the luxurious Queen Catherine. Naturally, Nathaniel endeavours to turn The Filthy Whore to the land of Hoopla girls but only manages to steer the dirty lady of ill repute galleon to Hell's Bucket; a notorious stretch of water where no ships dare go. Unimpressed with his navigational attempts, the salty sea dog crew cast him adrift to go slowly mad. Instead he is rescued by Chocki, an unpredictable half-Viking/half-shark. Their adventures are only just beginning… Nathaniel saves (read 'screws up a world record swimming attempt') Trina and falls in love. Then there's the ice monster. A seductive six-armed temptress. Her irate husband Mulligan the giant. Will Nathaniel ever find Hawaii? Will he ever find true love? Will he ever grow up?

Comment: A real missed opportunity, *Cabin Boy* supposedly mixes surreal comedy with bawdy humour. It attempts a cross between Pee-wee Herman and Monty Python - the naive man-boy's bizarre encounters amidst deliberately self-referential and unrealistic sets. It should work - it's set in the past but contains anachronisms (chocolate milk, tins of beer, microwaves), the dialogue is based upon contemporary scientific thinking (talking about Chocki's chromosomes), the sets are great and the lighting extreme in a comic book style. Likewise, the knowingly camp effects are suited to the production - Nathaniel hallucinates a talking cupcake, mythical creatures come to life via blue screen or stop-frame and the ships are clearly models in well-lit sets. There are several references that pepper the film and for lovers of *Jason And The Argonauts* more similarities than entirely healthy (the living figurehead, Mulligan reprising the Talos role, the stop-motion ice creatures etc.). The problem is that it is just not funny - Chris Elliot, the central character, is less sympathetic than Pee-wee Herman and virtually beyond redemption. It doesn't say anything about the class system, the place of the rich or provide any worthwhile statement on anything. The plot just ends, the conclusion is unsatisfactory, it's less smutty than a *Carry On* film but tries to make up for that with gratuitous swearing and rewards someone irrefutably odious with a future of affluence. Still Steve Bartek provides a super score, the opening credits are nice, Russ Tamblyn is the finest half-Viking/half-shark offspring to grace cinema and at least it's all over quickly. *Cabin Boy* was a commercial failure on release, too weird for most (where have we heard that before?) and too average for anyone else.

The Verdict: 2/5

Batman Forever (1995)

Crew: Dir: Joel Schumacher, Prd: Tim Burton, Peter MacGregor-Scott, Scr: Lee Batchler, Janet Scott Batchler, Akiva Goldsman, 121 mins

Cast: Val Kilmer (Bruce Wayne/Batman), Tommy Lee Jones (Harvey Dent/ Harvey Two-Face), Jim Carrey (Edward Nygma/The Riddler), Nicole Kidman (Dr Chase Meridian), Chris O'Donnell (Dick Grayson/Robin)

Plot: Harvey Two-Face, psychotic coin-tossing criminal, has become obsessed with his arch-nemesis, Batman. No plan is too devious for this dual delinquent as his increasingly bizarre attempts to catch the dark knight see him raiding Gotham City's bank and even attempting a daring bomb heist at the circus. This later escapade results in the tragic demise of all but one of the Flying Graysons. The sole survivor, Dick, saves the day at deep personal loss. Enraged with vengeance, he seeks Two-Face's death but to do so requires the services of multimillionaire Bruce Wayne. Bruce too is having a tough time of it - he's got the hots for psychiatrist Dr Chase but she's unsure as to whether she wants to commit to him or the crime fighter. Then there's Edward Nygma. Edward is a brilliant but confused scientist who takes Bruce's rejection of his immersive entertainment technology to heart and reinvents himself as pun-meister supervillain The Riddler. When The Riddler joins forces with Two-Face, the denizens of Gotham City have their cerebral capacity hoovered up by Nygmatech's insidious infernal intellect incapacitator, and the prospects for a morally fortuitous conclusion seem remote.

Comment: Both Warner Brothers and Burton faced a Riddler-sized conun-drum when it came to the third of the *Batman* series. Burton had grown tired of large projects and was keen to pursue other ventures. The studios realised that Burton's reputation and name helped boost the films but were keen to produce something with a lighter tone – especially in response to the criticism of *Batman Returns*. So the solution was to make this a Tim Burton Production but hand the reins over to someone who could deliver the kind of frothy eye-candy that Warner Brothers sought. So after two dark fantasies, the *Batman* franchise returned to the neon drenched Day-Glo excesses of the Adam West series. Out went Keaton and in came Val Kilmer, complete with badly-timed puns and excruciating delivery. In came Robin, his adoption by Bruce Wayne harking back to the original comics. One little aside to Burton remains. When we see The Riddler, in the depths of Arkham Asylum (a link to both the Dark

Knight comics and HP Lovecraft), one of the white-coated observers asks him, "Dr Burton tells me you know who Batman is."

As a film this ain't great, but as camp excess it can do little wrong. No camera angle is left untilted. No scene is underlit. The colours are so intense they are headache-inducing. The only traces of depression lie in Batman's dreams of his parents' death which are detached and swift enough not to overwhelm the sense of fun. Instead of being a sequel to Tim Burton's *Batman* films this is almost as though they never happened, despite the familiar faces of Commissioner Gordon and Albert the butler. Gotham City has transformed from a huge brooding noir setting to a bigger glitzy circus, overbearing in gaudy kitsch trappings and gigantic statues.

Burton's characters are psychologically scarred misfits who turn to fetishism to externalise their feelings. Schumacher uses the process of dressing up to emphasise sexual identity rather that express their emotions. Almost invariably the film embraces the connection between machismo and homosexuality, the Dr Chase romance notwithstanding, to create a Felliniesque parade of gimp mask-wearing henchmen, heroes in rubber suits, bulging codpieces and double-entendre laden dialogue. Carrey is unbelievably camp when freed of the shackles of his day-to-day engineering job, mincing around like a drag queen. Ultimately this raises the film from tedium into entertainment although it's a decidedly brains-off kind. As shallow as a thin crust pizza but savoury nonetheless.

The Verdict: 3/5

James And The Giant Peach (1996)

Crew: Dir: Henry Selick, Prd: Denise Di Novi, Tim Burton, Scr: Karey Kirkpatrick, Jonathon Roberts, Steve Bloom, 79 mins

Cast: Paul Terry (James), Joanna Lumley (Spiker), Miriam Margolyes (Sponge), Pete Postlethwaite (Strange Old Man) with Simon Callow, Richard Dreyfus, Susan Sarandon, Jane Leeves, David Thewlis

Plot: Poor little James Henry Trotter. Having his parents brutally killed by an enormous rhinoceros was bad enough. Now it looks like he's got to spend his life doing unpleasant chores for Aunts Spiker and Sponge. He is even forced to eject his only friend, a spider, for fear of it being killed by the nasty hags. But one evening he meets a strange old man who gives him a carton filled with crocodile's tongues. Tragedy strikes and the tongues escape, one causing a peach to blossom on the gnarled dead tree that sits in his aunts' gnarled dead garden. And what a peach it is, swelling to enormous size and great profit for his entrepreneurial relatives. Not for long. The final renegade tongue finds its way into James' stomach and before you can say "Aaaaggghhh!" the peach rolls through the countryside, before launching of a cliff and into the sea. What a rush! And what's more, James now has companions, all ready to sail to New York City: a dapper monocled grasshopper, a cigar-smoking Brooklyn centipede, a motherly ladybird, an old glow-worm, a myopic paranoid earthworm and, yes, his spider, a sultry noirish femme fatale. They have many dangers to face if they are to find fame and freedom in the Big Apple, on a Giant Peach.

Comment: Roald Dahl's books have provided endless entertainment for children of all ages and have produced a surprising number of great films. The best of these (*Matilda*, *The Witches* and *James And The Giant Peach*) have benefited by retaining the sadistic and revolting aspects of Dahl's work as well as the fantastical and magical moments, which also reflects Burton's outlook. Spiker and Sponge are truly nasty. They not only treat James as a slave but enjoy their power and deliberately malnourish him. ("I've finished my chores", "What a coincidence, we've finished the dinner.") What's worse they mock his deceased parents and threaten him with the dreaded rhino. Their place in the film lies in the live action sequences that bookend the central, stop-frame animated journey but are no less fantastic. Their house is of fairy-tale evil and virtually colourless. They are grotesque caricatures of narcissism and repugnant ugliness (played with malignant vitriol by Lumley and Margolyes). When the animation kicks in the colours suddenly become magical and impossibly bright as befits the incredible journey. Unrestrained by the tight, gothic, internally logical (but perfectly balanced) world of *The Nightmare Before Christmas,* Selick creates a barrage of exciting and dynamic images: the scary mechanical shark with countless rows of rotating razor-sharp teeth, the flock of seagulls pulling the peach through the golden clouds and an arctic wasteland of ghost ships eerily quiet in the bleach white cold. The later scene sees the repentant drowsy centipede 'committing pesticide' to recover a compass from a pirate ship only to face Jack Skellington and his demon shipmates. Even more bizarre is James' dream, animated in a curious cut-out fashion similar to Selick's earlier experimental shorts. The only problem with *James And The Giant Peach* is a handful of Randy Newman songs, but at least the relentless visual imagination is put on overdrive during these numbers and pulls you through to the next enchanting scene. And, if you need to be told, stay until the credits have finished - it's worth the wait.

The Verdict: 5/5

What's This? Other Projects

Singles (1992)

Crew: Dir: Cameron Crowe

Cast: Bridget Fonda, Matt Dillon, Bill Pullman, Tim Burton

Plot: A group of friends and neighbours fall in and out of relationships with each other in search of that indefinable thing called love. If they can be bothered that is.

Comment: Cameron Crowe's feature is an amiable little romp through the lives and loves of a group of people in Seattle. A touch heavy in the soundtrack department, this is a pleasant enough way to pass 90 minutes or so. Sort of slacker lite, this laid-back (lots of direct to cameras, monologues and hip dialogue) film features Burton's big-screen cameo. His character, Brian, is a director who works at a singles' agency making videos for people seeking a partner. His contribution is two syllables long:

"Ten bucks extra and Brian will shoot your video."

"Twenty." (Brian)

"He doesn't even know me," protests Debbie.

"Debbie, he's only like the next Martin Scorsese." before he disappears, never to be seen again.

Adverts

Many directors have tried their hands at advertising and Burton has also made some that are typically eclectic. It is difficult to incorporate plot and characterisation while selling a product and still have change from 60 seconds, but therein lies the art of the ad.

Hollywood Chewing Gum (1998): Chewing gum brand that, unsurprisingly perhaps, does not originate from Hollywood but is popular in Europe. Burton's ad for the product is a real stormer known as The Gnome. Our hero, a plucky little gnome, tires of his job standing day and night in a garden and dreams of a better life. A quick shin over the garden wall and he's off, weaving between legs in a shopping mall, hiding in the shadows and eventually jumping on a passing car. Dropped off near his destination, he pounds his way through the undergrowth until he comes across a beautiful grotto with a bathing siren. Spurred on, he dives in as the camera tastefully pulls focus onto a packet of Hollywood Chewing Gum. Fast, funny and exciting, this bizarre little ad has music courtesy of prolific advert sound design wizard Claude Letessier.

Timex (2000): Currently the latest of Burton's advertising projects, the first of these proved so successful that a second was commissioned. Both are to plug Timex's easy-to-use watches and are chiaroscuro pieces with asides to *The Matrix* and *Blade Runner*. The second advert stars Lisa Marie hiding in a dummy warehouse while sinister operatives search for her whereabouts, decapitating dummies as they go. Impressive wirework kung-fu and a driving *Matrix*-style soundtrack make for invigorating if somewhat derivative viewing. Both adverts are available to view online at www.timex.com and include a brief documentary as well. Pack a decent modem or be prepared for an inevitable wait.

Stainboy

An absolute must, this is Tim Burton's online cartoon series, extending the character from his book *The Melancholy Death Of Oyster Boy And Other Stories*. For the cost of a local phone call you can have Stainboy on your desktop in a series of his bizarre and gory adventures. Written and directed by Burton these short (about three minutes or so) animations also feature the music of Danny Elfman. Facing the shocking Staregirl (and bringing very rough justice to the poor mite), Matchgirl (voiced by Lisa Marie) or Toxicboy he's never far from another gripping and cynical mission.

http://www.shockwave.com/bin/shockwave/entry.jsp?page=/minisites/stainboy/home.html

Burton Books And Bookmarks

The following is a selected bibliography of recommended reading.

Books By Burton

The Melancholy Death Of Oyster Boy & Other Stories by Tim Burton, William Morrow & Co, ISBN: 0688156819 - A collection of offbeat rhymes about misunderstood youth, this is a delightful and poignant little book. Filled with typically sketchy drawings and a Dr Seuss sense of the absurd this comes highly recommended.

The Nightmare Before Christmas by Tim Burton, ASIN: 0786810149

Tim Burton's Nightmare Before Christmas: A Pop-Up Book by Tim Burton, ASIN: 0453031323

Tim Burton's Nightmare Before Christmas: A Postcard Book, ASIN: 1561383406

Tim Burton's Nightmare Before Christmas: An Animated Flip Book by Tim Burton, ASIN: 1562827758

Tim Burton's Nightmare Before Christmas: A Novel by Daphne Skinner, Caroline Thompson, Tim Burton, Touchstone Pictures, ISBN: 1562825925

Books About Burton

Tim Burton: An Unauthorised Biography Of The Film-Maker by Ken Hanke, Renaissance Books, ISBN: 1580631622 - Readable, informative biography of the director.

Burton On Burton, ed Mark Salisbury, Faber & Faber, ISBN: 0571176704 - A collection of interviews with Burton covering his career up to *Mars Attacks!* Good, solid read with some well-chosen illustrations and informative passages.

Tim Burton: The Life And Films Of A Visionary Director by Helmut Merschmann, Titan Books, ISBN: 1840232080 - Profusely illustrated with screen shots, this book covers all the films up to *Sleepy Hollow* and is bizarrely categorised by theme.

Tim Burton A Child's Garden Of Nightmares, ed Paul A Woods, Plexus, ISBN: 0859653102

Books About Burton's Films

The Art Of Sleepy Hollow, Andrew Kevin Walker (Editor), Tim Burton (Introduction), Pocket Books, ISBN: 0671036572

Sleepy Hollow: Including The Classic Story By Washington Irving by Peter Lerangis, Tim Burton (Introduction), Pocket Books, ISBN: 0671036653

Tim Burton's Nightmare Before Christmas: The Film, The Art, The Vision by Frank Thompson, Hyperion, ISBN: 156282774X

Mars Attacks! The Art Of The Movie by Karen R Jones, Ballantine Books, ISBN: 0345409981

Batman: The Official Book Of The Movie by John Marriott, Hamlyn, ISBN: 0660565874

Batman Returns: The Official Movie Book by Michael Singer, Hamlyn, ISBN:0600574938

DVD

Big budgets, big films, big sounds. Given the choice DVD is your only real option for home entertainment, although the cinema is the proper place to appreciate Burton's films. At the time of writing, all his features are available on DVD with the exception, tragically, of *Ed Wood* (and, of course, *Planet Of The Apes*). Those with multi-region players face a few tough choices: PAL picture quality is generally better than NTSC but the extra features vary depending on territory.

Batman - Nice transfer but typically frills-free. (D012000)

Batman Forever - Lovely colours, anamorphic transfer but the composition feels cramped. (D015100)

Batman Returns - Another 'extras-light' disc which, again, you need to buy Region 1 or from France if you want it uncut. (D015000)

Beetlejuice - Nothing to shout about in the way of extras but there is the option of watching the film with just the soundtrack, which seems like a nice idea, but is so 'stop-start' without the dialogue you'd be hard pressed to make it to the end. (D011785)

Edward Scissorhands - Nice transfer, mini documentary and some production drawings. Bizarre 4.0 surround but the highlight is two (count 'em) commentaries, one from Burton and another from Elfman. As the film is cut in the UK, perhaps the best place to buy is in France where you get all the advantages of a PAL picture and none of the cuts. (01867DVD)

James And The Giant Peach - Stick with the Region 1 Special Edition, you know it's worth it. (P8870DVD)

Mars Attacks! - A few trailers and another 'music only' option accompany the standard spread of biogs etc. Sadly the menu option of the soundtrack in Martian rather than English is just a little joke. (D014480)

The Nightmare Before Christmas - Do not touch the general release Region 2 disc, it's only got the film! Instead try the Region 1 Special Edition that features *Vincent* and *Frankenweenie,* deleted scenes, makings of and more information than you can comfortably handle. Essential. (D034524 or Reg 1 ASIN: 6305949980)

Pee-wee's Big Adventure - Currently only on Region 1 NTSC, this features a running commentary from Burton and Reubens, deleted scenes and 5.1 sound. (ASIN: 0790749408)

Sleepy Hollow - Reasonable documentary and some nice menus complement a great transfer complete with running commentary from Burton. Those of you with expensive sound set-ups (you lucky devils) should perhaps check out the Region 1 version which has DTS sound. (P8986DVD)

Videos

Below is a list of UK available videos. NTSC copies can easily be obtained through your favourite online video retailer. Timings are for PAL VHS versions with BBFC imposed cuts noted in brackets.

Batman (1989) S012000 121mins 4s
Batman (Widescreen) (1989) S012546 121mins 4s
Batman Returns (1992) S015000 121mins 4s (9s cut)
Batman Returns (Widescreen) (1992) S012691 121mins 4s (9s cut)
Beetlejuice (1988) S011785 88mins 13s
Ed Wood (1994) CC7842 121mins 18s
Edward Scissorhands (Special Edition) (1991) 01867CS 100mins 24s (15s cut)
Mars Attacks! S014480 101mins 21s
Mars Attacks! (Widescreen) S015424 101mins 21s
Pee-wee's Big Adventure (1985) S011523 87mins 20s
Sleepy Hollow (1999) P8986S 100mins 55s

World Wide Web

There are scores of sites out there for those thirsty for more information. Some specialise in more speculative stories such as upcoming projects, whilst others concentrate on the body of work already completed. Below are sites that all come highly recommended, there are many more.

The Official Tim Burton Page - www.timburton.com - At the time of writing this contains a picture of Stainboy and the promise of more to come.

The Tim Burton Collective - www.timburtoncollective.com - Crisp and fast site offering lots to read (over 150 articles from newspapers alone) and all the latest news. Economic design belies the fact that there is a lot to be found here including plenty of multimedia content and even the Timex adverts to download. Fab.

Tim Burton - http://home.acadia.net/userpages/joel/timburton/ - Nicely designed page in moody black, white and purple. Rich with content but hasn't been updated in a while, which is a shame.

Mars Attacks! (Official Site) - www.marsattacks.com - Very silly site with lots of colour and a few shockwave games. The shooting gallery is totally pointless but hysterically funny.

Dan's Definitive Tim Burton Page (aka Tim Burton: Auteur or Marketing Concept) -www.euronet.nl/users/bramb/dan/burton/title.html - A little old (it covers up to *Mars Attacks!*) but interesting précis of Burton's career looking at the contradiction between money and art. Follow the train of thought by either thematic (expressionism, horror films, the outsider) or chronological means.

Tim Burton FAQs - www.rit.edu/~elnppr/faqs/tbfaq.html - Short but sweet page of snippets and rumours about Burton.

...that website about Tim Burton - www.zipworld.com.au/~adandnat/burton/ - Nice, regularly updated site from Australia with wobbly graphics and some unusual use of html.

If you would like to contact the authors, you can visit their website at: www.colinandmitch.com.

The Essential Library

Build up your library with new titles every month

Alfred Hitchcock by Paul Duncan

More than 20 years after his death, Alfred Hitchcock is still a household name, most people in the Western world have seen at least one of his films, and he popularised the action movie format we see every week on the cinema screen. He was both a great artist and dynamite at the box office. This book examines the genius and enduring popularity of one of the most influential figures in the history of the cinema!

Stanley Kubrick by Paul Duncan

Kubrick's work, like all masterpieces, has a timeless quality. His vision is so complete, the detail so meticulous, that you believe you are in a three-dimensional space displayed on a two-dimensional screen. He was commercially successful because he embraced traditional genres like War (*Paths Of Glory*, *Full Metal Jacket*), Crime (*The Killing*), Science Fiction (*2001*), Horror (*The Shining*) and Love (*Barry Lyndon*). At the same time, he stretched the boundaries of film with controversial themes: underage sex (*Lolita*); ultra violence (*A Clockwork Orange*); and erotica (*Eyes Wide Shut*).

Orson Welles by Martin Fitzgerald

The popular myth is that after the artistic success of *Citizen Kane* it all went downhill from there for Orson Welles, that he was some kind of fallen genius. Yet, despite overwhelming odds, he went on to make great Films Noirs like *The Lady From Shanghai* and *Touch Of Evil*. He translated Shakespeare's work into films with heart and soul (*Othello*, *Chimes At Midnight*, *Macbeth*), and he refused to take the bite out of modern literature, giving voice to bitterness, regret and desperation in *The Magnificent Ambersons* and *The Trial*. Far from being down and out, Welles became one of the first cutting-edge independent filmmakers.

Film Noir by Paul Duncan

The laconic private eye, the corrupt cop, the heist that goes wrong, the femme fatale with the rich husband and the dim lover - these are the trademark characters of Film Noir. This book charts the progression of the Noir style as a vehicle for film-makers who wanted to record the darkness at the heart of American society as it emerged from World War to the Cold War. As well as an introduction explaining the origins of Film Noir, seven films are examined in detail and an exhaustive list of over 500 Films Noirs are listed.

The Essential Library

Build up your library with new titles every month

Film Directors:

Jane Campion (£2.99)	**John Carpenter** (£3.99)
Jackie Chan (£2.99)	**Joel & Ethan Coen** (£3.99)
David Cronenberg (£3.99)	**Terry Gilliam** (£2.99)
Alfred Hitchcock (£3.99)	**Krzysztof Kieslowski** (£2.99)
Stanley Kubrick (£2.99)	**Sergio Leone** (£3.99)
David Lynch (£3.99)	**Brian De Palma** (£2.99)
Sam Peckinpah (£2.99)	**Ridley Scott** (£3.99)
Orson Welles (£2.99)	**Billy Wilder** (£3.99)
Steven Spielberg (£3.99)	

Film Genres:

Film Noir (£3.99)	**Hong Kong Heroic Bloodshed** (£2.99)
Horror Films (£3.99)	**Slasher Movies**(£3.99)
Spaghetti Westerns (£3.99)	**Vampire Films** (£2.99)
Blaxploitation Films (£3.99)	

Film Subjects:

Laurel & Hardy (£3.99)	**Marx Brothers** (£3.99)
Steve McQueen (£2.99)	**Marilyn Monroe** (£3.99)
The Oscars® (£3.99)	**Filming On A Microbudget** (£3.99)
Bruce Lee (£3.99)	

TV:

Doctor Who (£3.99)

Literature:

Cyberpunk (£3.99)	**Philip K Dick** (£3.99)
Hitchhiker's Guide (£3.99)	**Noir Fiction** (£2.99)
Terry Pratchett (£3.99)	**Sherlock Holmes** (£3.99)

Ideas:

Conspiracy Theories (£3.99)	**Nietzsche** (£3.99)
Feminism (£3.99)	

History:

Alchemy & Alchemists (£3.99)	**The Crusades** (£3.99)

Available at all good bookstores, or send a cheque to: **Pocket Essentials (Dept TB), 18 Coleswood Rd, Harpenden, Herts, AL5 1EQ, UK**. Please make cheques payable to 'Oldcastle Books.' Add 50p postage & packing for each book in the UK and £1 elsewhere.

US customers can send $6.95 plus $1.95 postage & packing for each book to: **Trafalgar Square Publishing, PO Box 257, Howe Hill Road, North Pomfret, Vermont 05053, USA**. e-mail: tsquare@sover.net

Customers worldwide can order online at **www.pocketessentials.com**.

The Essential Library

Build up your library with new titles every month

Tim Burton by Colin Odell & Michelle Le Blanc, £3.99

Tim Burton makes films about outsiders on the periphery of society. His heroes are psychologically scarred, perpetually naive and childlike, misunderstood or unintentionally disruptive. They upset convential society and morality. Even his villains are rarely without merit - circumstance blurs the divide between moral fortitude and personal action. But most of all, his films have an aura of the fairytale, the fantastical and the magical.

Film Music by Paul Tonks, £3.99

From *Ben-Hur* to *Star Wars* and *Psycho* to *Scream*, film music has played an essential role in such genre-defining classics. Making us laugh, cry, and jump with fright, it's the manipulative tool directors cannot do without. The turbulent history, the ever-changing craft, the reclusive or limelight-loving superstars, the enthusiastic world of fandom surrounding it, and the best way to build a collection, is all streamlined into a user-friendly guide for buffs and novices alike.

Woody Allen (Revised & Updated Edition) by Martin Fitzgerald, £3.99

Woody Allen: Neurotic. Jewish. Funny. Inept. Loser. A man with problems. Or so you would think from the characters he plays in his movies. But hold on. Allen has written and directed 30 films. He may be a funny man, but he is also one of the most serious American film-makers of his generation. This revised and updated edition includes *Sweet And Lowdown* and *Small Time Crooks*.

American Civil War by Phil Davies, £3.99

The American Civil War, fought between North and South in the years 1861-1865, was the bloodiest and most traumatic war in American history. Rival visions of the future of the United States faced one another across the battlefields and, as in any civil war, families and friends were bitterly divided by the conflict. Phil Davies looks at the deep-rooted causes of the war, so much more complicated than the simple issue of slavery.

American Indian Wars by Howard Hughes, £3.99

At the beginning of the 1840s the proud tribes of the North American Indians looked across the plains at the seemingly unstoppable expansion of the white man's West. During the decades of conflict that followed, as the new world pushed onward, the Indians saw their way of life disappear before their eyes. Over the next 40 years they clung to a dream of freedom and a continuation of their traditions, a dream that was repeatedly shattered by the whites.

Available at all good bookstores, or send a cheque to: **Pocket Essentials (Dept TB), 18 Coleswood Rd, Harpenden, Herts, AL5 1EQ, UK**. Please make cheques payable to 'Oldcastle Books.' Add 50p postage & packing for each book in the UK and £1 elsewhere.

US customers can send $6.95 plus $1.95 postage & packing for each book to: **Trafalgar Square Publishing, PO Box 257, Howe Hill Road, North Pomfret, Vermont 05053, USA**. e-mail: tsquare@sover.net

Customers worldwide can order online at **www.pocketessentials.com**.